When My Mother No Longer Knew My Name

A SON'S "COURSE" IN "RATIONAL" CAREGIVING

STEPHEN L. GOLDSTEIN, Ph.D.

Grid Press   Ashland, OR

WHEN MY MOTHER NO LONGER KNEW MY NAME
©2012 STEPHEN L. GOLDSTEIN, PH.D

Published by Grid Press
(An imprint of L&R Publishing, LLC)

Grid Press
PO Box 3531
Ashland, OR 97520
www.hellgatepress.com

Editing: Harley B. Patrick
Interior design: Sasha Kincaid
Cover design: L. Redding

Library of Congress Cataloging-in-Publication Data

Goldstein, Stephen L., 1943-
 When my mother no longer knew my name : a son's "course" in "rational" caregiving / Stephen L. Goldstein.
    p. cm.
 ISBN 978-1-55571-701-8
 1. Older people--Care. 2. Older parents. I. Title.
 HV1451.G65 2012
 649.8084'6--dc23

                    2011050614

Printed and bound in the United States of America
First edition 10 9 8 7 6 5 4 3 2

To the memory of my mother,
Sylvia K. Goldstein,
who gave me life, devoted her life to me,
and let me care for her,
even when she no longer knew
who I was

CONTENTS

INTRODUCTION

*It is our choices, Harry, that show what we
truly are, far more than our abilities.
–J. K. Rowling*

There is already a caregiving crisis in the U.S. — too few family members willing and able to care for their parents in their home, too many aging parents in need — and it's only going to get worse. As the nation's population continues to age, more and more seniors will need help with daily living. Typically, they aren't acutely ill, but are frail and failing, limited in what they can do and where they can go. Slowly but surely, their condition gets worse, not better. Tens of millions of us will be affected because we will either need others to care for us or we will need to care for someone else.

Unfortunately, the nation is in denial. Family caregiving is low on the totem pole of priorities and never discussed publicly with the urgency it merits. It was barely mentioned during the months of debate over health system reform. The new law provided for only a voluntary, long-term care policy with minimal benefits and a token daily payout — but even that has been scrapped because it proved unworkable. We can't possibly build enough public or private facilities to accommodate the additional millions of Americans who soon will need care. Insurance companies will not be able to write enough affordable policies paying enough in benefits to defray all the costs we'll face as families and as a nation. And no government program or programs will be able to meet the demand for services.

The *only* solution to our eldercare crisis is obvious: We need to become a nation of family caregivers. I want to urge others to open their hearts, their homes, and their wallets if necessary to their parents in their declining years, even though it is difficult, challenging, and at times depressing. I also want to show families how they can prepare for the roles and responsibilities of living with and caring for family members, especially their aging and frail relatives, many of whom will suffer from dementia, Alzheimer's, and similar conditions. I believe people should be institutionalized only as the absolute last resort—when they need round-the-clock, skilled care and caring for them at home would be detrimental to them. It's not about money; it's about *neshoma* (Yiddish for soul). Whatever you call them— assisted-living facilities being perhaps the most palatable — the unvarnished truth is even the most exclusive and expensive of them are human warehouses. Assuming there's good blood between family members, it really does run thicker than even the purest water of compassionate strangers. If home is where the heart is, it's surely where family members deserve to be when they need care, especially in the final years of their life.

Caregiving isn't just for women. Most people are shocked to learn about 34 percent of all caregivers in the U.S. are men. By one estimate that's 14.5 million men; by another, as high as 22 million. Make sure all the men in your family play a prominent role in your family caregiving.

I especially want to give hope to mothers and fathers whose sons are their likeliest caregiver. A commonly accepted misperception in America today is that if you want to be cared for in your old age, you'd better have a daughter. Traditionally, a son is thought to be lost to his own family, co-opted by his wife's. Even my mother believed it; at least, as a child, I recall her saying, in addition to my brother and me, she would have liked to have had at least one daughter to remain close to her.

Happily, I proved my mother wrong. In 1998, just before her 80th birthday, I invited her to move in with me. And during the 10-plus years we lived together, she discovered I cared about and for her at least as well as any two daughters combined. My brother was *always* "there" for her, too.

The saddest words I've ever heard were repeated to me when my mother was in the hospital, in a rehab facility, and under the care of private duty caregivers at our home. Again and again, shocked professionals told me when they contacted the relatives of people in their care to tell them they were in the hospital or in a nursing home, too often their response was, "Call me when they die."

I realize every family is different, of course. Not everyone has had a "giving" parent or parents—or is on good terms with them. Caregiving at home is disruptive. I would be the last person to romanticize the experience or the commitment it takes to adjust to eldercare. Not everyone has the extra space I had to accommodate a parent or parents, let alone the emotional reserve. An elderly parent's needs become greater, more complex, more costly, and more taxing over time.

But more than anything, I want to make America a nation of rational, responsible caregivers — people who plan ahead for the likely day when they or someone in their family can no longer care for themselves, partially or totally. Successful and effective caregiving isn't an emotional or knee-jerk reaction to crises. It's the result of thinking through alternative scenarios to deal effectively with different circumstances, long before they arise.

Discover how caregiving can be a joy or you'll never be able to bear the sorrow, especially as you watch the parent upon whom you depended during your whole life slip away from reality— and you.

Strange as it may sound, I also

want to make America a nation of joyful caregivers. But how can I possibly write joy and caregiving in the same phrase? How can I suggest there could be anything upbeat about caring for a parent who no longer knew my name? I experienced it.

It took me four-and-a-half years and the sadness of living with my mother who had dementia to discover the "joy" of "caregiving", and it took me more than two years to write a book to relive it, tell my story, and share practical tips to show others how they too can become joyful in the most unlikely of circumstances. It isn't the sudden joy of seeing a newborn baby or graduating from college or of taking an exotic trip or winning the lottery or of any of the experiences people typically think lift their spirits. However powerful it may be, that kind of upbeat feeling attached to a given experience fades. The joy from caregiving is more like bliss — a stereophonic, profound and lasting feeling, a unique emotion that comes from giving your all for someone else while expecting absolutely nothing in return.

Overwhelming positives outweigh any and all the negatives of caring for someone whose life is slipping away. For me, nothing is more gratifying than knowing I gave my mother the best care she could possibly have gotten in the last years of her life — absolutely nothing! I cannot imagine not having done this for her. You don't know what love is until you've changed your mother's or father's diaper, survived the shock when they no longer know your name, or have spent time holding the hand of, and talking to, someone with dementia, whether they appear to understand what you're saying or not. In the end, one of the rewards of caring for someone else is discovering a part of yourself you might never have known.

As personal as my observations and experiences are, they contain at total of 75 tips filled with valuable perspectives and practical advice from which everyone may benefit. There are lots of things I would have

The odds are unpaid family members will have to provide most in-home care. But, because there may come a time when paid professionals will need to assist them, it is never too early to weigh the pros and cons of taking out long-term, in-home care insurance. There's a case to be made for getting it — or not. The care someone needs may at first be minimal, lasting just a few hours, and the cost may be manageable. But the bill for 24/7 care can be astronomical. When my mother needed round-the-clock care, we paid $400 per day out-of-pocket, just for home-health aides. She had decided against taking out an insurance policy. She only needed one-on-one, professional assistance for a matter of weeks. But it still added up quickly. If she had paid thousands of dollars in insurance premiums for years, it wouldn't have been cost-effective for us. In retrospect, we took a calculated risk and made the right choice. But we may have been more lucky than wise. We could have faced a major financial drain. The lesson is to be prepared: Research your options and plan ahead, especially for the unexpected, which can almost be guaranteed to occur. And most important of all, know where the money for long-term care is going to come from if it's needed.

wanted to know and might have done differently. There are many things I learned on-the-job and that could *only* be learned by trial-and-error. I've written my reflections and tips hoping they might help current and future caregivers avoid unnecessary mistakes.

My experiences of caring for and providing care for my mother were the defining moments of my life. They are written entirely from memory. While she was alive, I didn't want to keep a diary because I didn't want to treat her living with me like a laboratory experiment. And I didn't want to do anything, even subliminally, thinking it would make good copy for an eventual publication. Nonetheless, the writer in me knew the day would come when I would simply *have to* write something, both for myself and others. I made mental notes.

Ten years is a long time in anyone's life. When I invited my mother to move in with me neither of us had any idea how long we would live together or which of us would die first. As the years progressed, she became more and more dependent upon me, and I gradually made adjustments to my personal and professional lives I never dreamed I'd have to: My whole life for four-and-a-half years revolved around taking care of her. Reliving those moments is my way of turning my abiding grief over her loss into a celebration of the unconditional love I found in myself for her — for love, pure and simple, trite as it may sound, is what *real* caregiving ultimately is. My decision to invite my mother to live with me was the best thing I've ever done in my life — an unqualified joy. A similar experience can be equally transforming and rewarding for everyone.

1

DETERMINING YOUR "CAREGIVING READINESS": *PRE-ASSESSMENT*

An ethic of care rests on the premise of nonviolence — that no one should be hurt.
– Carol Gilligan

Sooner or later, directly or indirectly, every American will be involved in caregiving. It's never too soon, or too late, to test yourself to see how well prepared you are for what may turn out to be the most challenging role of your life, but which you probably never thought you'd have to play.

This self-test is designed so you can get the most out of the chapters that follow. Take it before you read them to benchmark how you rate yourself as a caregiver. Then, pay special attention to the chapters and tips which offer advice on areas in which you see yourself needing help and perspective. Take the test again after you finish the entire book to chart the progress you've made. I hope in the course of your reading you will have transformed yourself into a ready-and-able, informed caregiver.

After you finish the book and retake the test, go to my blog, www.rationalcaregiving.blogspot.com, for updates and information, as well as to email me your comments and questions.

Caregivers need all the help they can get facing a reality they could never have imagined for their own good and their family member's well-being. Without a doubt, being able personally to nurture parents in their declining years is a joy. But it comes at a high price: throwing out all inhibitions, prejudices, perceived limitations, expectations — and facing having to do things you never thought you'd have to deal with.

Honest parental caregivers know you've gotta do what you've gotta do, no matter what. Knowing I was writing my reflections on caregiving, a female friend of mine confided in me she had to change her father's diaper; a male friend shared his experience having to clean his wheelchair-bound father-in-law when he couldn't get to the bathroom in time.

There is no single caregiving script to follow. No single book can tell you everything you need to know, nor will there ever be one. Every parent-patient is different. Too many authors and professionals sugarcoat the challenges of being a parental caregiver or deal with them unrealistically. Ultimately, you will be the best judge of your fitness for assuming a role which is sure to change your life — way more even than being a parent. You need to begin by starkly facing reality — by looking yourself in the mirror and assessing yourself for the job.

Determining your "Caregiver Readiness" will help you benchmark where you see yourself in terms of the attitudes and responsibilities all caregivers need to have. There are no right or wrong answers, of course. Be totally frank and honest. You're only kidding yourself if you aren't and harming your chances of being the best caregiver you can be. Who knows? You may discover you already are, or are potentially, the consummate caregiver — or you are perfectly willing to put in the effort to become one.

Scoring Your "Caregiver Readiness"

On a scale from 0 (not at all) to 10 (absolutely), circle your score in response to each of the following statements:

....

1. I have thought through all the pros and cons of assuming the responsibility for caregiving 0 1 2 3 4 5 6 7 8 9 10

Before you score yourself, divide a sheet of paper into two vertical columns. Mark one Pros and under it list everything you can think of that would make you *want* to take responsibility for caregiving. Under Cons, list everything you can imagine that would make you *not want* to become a caregiver. For example, in what column(s) would you put how you feel about the people for whom you might be caring? If you hate your mother, you'd be in for a bumpy ride unless you can harness your negatives. You need to be very clear about how you score this benchmark. Unless your family member is clearly fading fast, your caregiving may extend into months or years. Are you willing to take one day at a time for however long it may be? If you don't give yourself a 10 here, you may be taking on a commitment which will potentially ruin your life and shortchange your family member.

What would you be willing to do to improve your score?

_____

_____

_____

_____

2. I am willing to make caregiving my number one priority, when and if the need arises 0 1 2 3 4 5 6 7 8 9 10

Before you determine your score, write down all the priorities in your life, from major to minor. Where would you place caregiving?

What would you be willing to do to improve your score?

_____

_____

_____

_____

**3. I am willing to discuss all the issues involved in my role
as caregiver with all of my family members who need, or
may need, my help** 0 1 2 3 4 5 6 7 8 9 10

Before you give yourself a 10 or less, list everyone you
need to talk with, as well as what issues you need to
discuss and what questions you need to ask and answer. Your
conversation needs to be no-holds-barred. For example,
you should address everything from how others see you as
caregiver to under what circumstances you might end your
role and place your family member in a nursing home or
other facility or under someone else's care.

What would you be willing to do to improve your score?

_____

_____

_____

_____

**4. I am willing to provide a separate living space for my
family member within my home** 0 1 2 3 4 5 6 7 8 9 10

Score yourself only after you ask yourself if *you* would
want to live in the space you would make available to your
family member. Are you prepared to redecorate it as your
family member might want it? Are you willing to go so far as
to add additional space onto your home if necessary — or
even move into a new house to accommodate her needs?
How willing are you to make *your* home feel welcoming?

What would you be willing to do to improve your score?

_____

_____

_____

_____

5.   I will see to it that all necessary papers (living will, healthcare surrogate, will, durable power of attorney, etc.) are executed by my family member(s) to ensure I am able to carry out my role as caregiver 0 1 2 3 4 5 6 7 8 9 10

There is nothing perfunctory about signing such important papers. Before you determine your score, think of the profound issues that creating and signing these few papers will raise. You will be asking your family members to put in writing who gets what from their estate, as well as when a machine keeping them alive would be shut off — or not.

What would you be willing to do to improve your score?

_____

_____

_____

_____

6.   I understand I can't be a caregiver by myself, and I need to create my own support system to help me ....
0 1 2 3 4 5 6 7 8 9 10

Before you rate yourself, list all of the current needs of your family member(s), as well as others you think are likely. Next, list all of the things you can think of you may need to do as a caregiver. Then, underline all of the things you believe *only* you can and should do. Next, make a list of people who might make up your support system. Next to their names put the responsibilities you believe they could handle exclusively or share. For example, next to someone's name you might suggest she commit to taking your family member to doctors' appointments or giving you a night off or taking your place at home while you go shopping. You may list the same responsibility next to more than one name. Do you have more needs than names (whoops!), or the reverse (lucky you!)?

What would you be willing to do to improve your score?

_____

_____

_____

_____

7. I am willing to plan for the financial resources to cover my family member's caregiving needs ....
0 1 2 3 4 5 6 7 8 9 10

Caregiving is costly both in time and money. Before you give yourself a 10, make a list of all the caregiving scenarios you can think of (your family member completely at home, possibly needing to go to a rehab facility, eventually choosing to go into a nursing home, whatever). Then, write down the financial implications of each alternative. List all available financial resources. For example, next to your at-home scenario, consider the possible cost of having to bring in temporary or long-term outside help. Compare the costs and benefits of long-term health insurance. Consider the cost-benefit of someone in your family not working, but making caregiving his full-time job. If your potential support system is extensive, consider actually pooling resources and paying a family member to provide care, instead of working elsewhere.

What would you be willing to do to improve your score?

_____

_____

_____

_____

8. I am willing to create "a family caregiving circle" after conferring with other family members ....
0 1 2 3 4 5 6 7 8 9 10

I hope you would rate yourself a 10 at this point, because that's really where you need to be in your thinking. Once you have determined (1) what your family member's caregiving needs are and are likely to become, (2) what your responsibilities and needs are, (3) who the members of your support group are, (4) what you think you can and should depend upon others for, and (5) what the cost of caregiving is likely to be, develop a DRAFT written plan you discuss with everyone potentially involved in your caregiving circle.

What would you be willing to do to improve your score?

_____

_____

_____

_____

9. I am willing to be an advocate for my family members so they get the care to which they are entitled ....
0 1 2 3 4 5 6 7 8 9 10

Before you circle a number, ask yourself if you have the stamina, smarts, and diplomatic skills to ensure your family member always receives the care she deserves and is entitled to. For example, are you willing to become thoroughly familiar with the fine print detailing what insurance policies cover and don't cover, even before you may need to file a claim? Do you have the time to stay up-to-date on policy changes and alternatives? Forewarned is forearmed. Negotiating the labyrinth of prescription drug formularies can be frustrating — and costly. Most of all, are you willing to speak up to doctors and other health care professionals to ensure they are caring for your family member in the best possible way — and keeping you informed about options and decisions you need to weigh? You'll need to do all of the above, and more, and still keep your cool, "speaking softly, but carrying a big stick," to be most effective. How well do you think you can do the job?

What would you be willing to do to improve your score?

_____

_____

_____

_____

10. I am prepared to see to it my family member receives appropriate medical and dental services and attention..................................... 0 1 2 3 4 5 6 7 8 9 10

Assuring proper medical attention for an aging family member, especially one with dementia or similar condition, is obviously crucial for her well-being. It's sometimes far more difficult than you might imagine, however. Going to doctor's and dentist's appointments is easy, though it obviously takes time you and others in your caregiving circle will have to make available. Even after you've taken time off from work, your family member may decide he doesn't want to leave the house to keep an appointment. She may even tell you she doesn't want to see anymore doctors or dentists. You can't allow them to harm themselves by refusing the care they need. If you absolutely can't get them to a doctor or dentist, you may need to find a way to bring medical services into your home, for which you may have to pay out-of-pocket. Be prepared, and understand that you absolutely cannot shirk such an important responsibility. You've got to guarantee they'll get the care they need — and score a 10 here!

What would you be willing to do to improve your score?

_____

_____

_____

_____

Total all your scores to get your "Caregiver Readiness"
_____ out of 100

Judging your "Caregiver Readiness"

On a scale of 0 (terrible) to 10 (great)

. . . .

How do *you* feel about your score? **0 1 2 3 4 5 6 7 8 9 10**

Ways to interpret your score:

Of course, your total score is an obvious way to benchmark how prepared and successful you are likely to be as a caregiver. But far more important are your 10 individual scores and what you would be willing to do to improve each of them.

I would contend your attitude toward caregiving is more important than anything else: Someone committed to giving it his all will overcome any difficulty or obstacle. Someone begrudgingly caregiving will put herself through a nightmare. Set yourself up for success: More than anything else, adopt a positive attitude to caregiving, before you commit to it.

2

GETTING US *BOTH* PSYCHED
FOR MY MOTHER'S MOVING IN

The distance is nothing;
it is only the first step that is difficult.
– Madame Du Deffand

On my mother's 79th birthday, I began *secretly* to plot. I came to the conclusion it was the perfect time for us to live together, precisely because from all outward appearances there was no need for her to do so. She was in good health and living independently; but at a gut level, I just *felt* she should no longer be living alone. Plus, as a trends analyst and forecaster, I had read or observed that once people turn 80, they begin a slow, natural decline.

I wanted my mother to move in to avoid a crisis in our lives. I didn't want to get a call from one of her neighbors, telling me she had fallen, broken her hip, and had been lying helplessly on the floor unattended for hours. She was a strong, determined individual. She raised a family, was in business and cared for my invalid father. She was always there for others. I dreaded a scenario where I would have to tell her she could no longer live alone, drive,

Get your family member(s) to move in with you before they need care so you can all act assertively. Spare them the public humiliation of no longer being able to live on their own. If you don't, all of you will likely become victims of circumstances.

or make choices for herself. I could picture the look of rage on her face, her clenched teeth, and her characteristic, fierce shaking of her right fist. I was determined to avoid such menacing at all costs and to spare her any humiliation.

As though you were signing an unbreakable contract, tell your family member or members exactly how you see your lives evolving together. I made the mistake of keeping my planning to myself. And I regret not having shared it, because it would have put to rest any doubts my mother might have had about her future. Explain the extent and limits of your commitment to being a caregiver, if there are any. Come to a shared understanding of what the future may hold for all of you. For example, agree to the conditions under which you would opt for a nursing home or other facility, or decide never to do so. Most of all, let your family members know they are safe with you and you will always put their interests first — assuming they are and you will, of course. That overall assurance I did give my mother, over and over again. And I could see from the relief in her expression it meant everything to her. I just never discussed the details of sharing our lives and, if need be, caring for her.

When I decided to invite my mother to live with me, I had no idea I would eventually become her caregiver or a clue about how my life would completely change. She was full of energy when she arrived a year after my plotting began, just before her 80th birthday.

If I thought about what might happen in the future, it was a fast-forward simply to my mother's dying. I never considered the extent of my investment in her needing long-term care. I always imagined I would simply go into her room one morning to discover she had died quietly in her sleep. I never wanted her to suffer or experience the indignity of slowly deteriorating. It never occurred to me there would be any time between her being strong and independent and eventually dying. Never for a nanosecond did I think I would gradually become a round-the-clock provider and supervisor of her care and my entire life would revolve around her needs — so much so that for several years I rarely left my house during the day and almost never went out at night.

Imagine every scenario of your life and how it would change if you became a caregiver to someone in your home. I kept a tally of the plusses and minuses in my head. Review the two columns you made answering the first statement when you determined your "Caregiver Readiness." Reconsider all the positives and negatives you thought of, especially if you're on the verge of making a commitment. Are there more considerations you need to add or others you'd like to delete? Do you need to recalculate your score?

At first, our living together appeared to me to be just a matter of combining households. But even so, I had to rearrange my thinking before I could rearrange my living space and accept the fact of her moving in. Intellectually, I thought about various ways my life would change. I would no longer be able to invite friends to visit because I would no longer have a guest room. But I dismissed my concern, because I rarely had overnight guests anyway. I would no longer be able to make changes to my house, or even buy furniture, on my own. My mother had very strong, and good, taste and would have been offended — make that furious — if I left her out of any decision-making. What might have at first appeared to be any negative consideration turned into a plus on balance, once I mulled it over.

In the end, no matter what scenario I replayed, nothing I was losing really seemed to matter. But everything we would be gaining appeared overwhelmingly positive.

Looking back on how we *both* got psyched for living together, I've realized unconsciously I followed a discernible process, though once we were *actually* in the same space, we were flying blind. Our shared script was up for grabs — at times, anybody's guess. But had I not first had a multi-part plan, I doubt our arrangement would have worked out as well as it did.

Follow a three-step process to get psyched for caregiving: First, imagine. Second, test. Third, bite the bullet. It worked for me — and my mother.

First, absolutely nothing was more important to me than ensuring my mother's independence and dignity were preserved in her later years. But I was *only* able to handle what eventually became my total commitment to doing something about it because I had made a conscious, ironclad, irreversible decision before I even broached the subject with her: Our living arrangement would be for the rest of our natural lives. Nothing, absolutely nothing, would ever lead me to tell her she had to move out — even if our life together turned out to be a living hell.

To reach my conclusion, I reran hypothetical scenarios of our living together again and again in my mind, until emotionally and rationally, it *felt* absolutely, positively *right* for us to be together. If I had any doubts, all I had to do was picture her hypothetically packing up, hurt and vulnerable, leaving me. And I couldn't imagine ever inflicting such deep pain and anguish on her, or feeling my share of it. After I don't know how many replays, with a definitive, unbearable scenario ingrained in my imagination, I *knew* I would never tell her to leave in real life.

Second, to test my level of certainty, I simulated our being together. Of course, my mother had no idea what I was doing. But at every opportunity, I created likely situations to give me a feel for what having her with me 24/7 would be like. The November before she moved in, she had cataract surgery. Seizing on a perfect dry-run moment, I invited her to stay with me to recover for a few days. Though three days does not a lifetime make, I was very comfortable with our concentrated time together. She was in good humor; we didn't argue and she wasn't in my way. Most important, she was genuinely glad to be with me. In my imagination, I ran a movie of our life together, simulating other scenes — daily meals, evenings, and holidays. All of them appeared workable, even joyful. My mother was a great cook and always made holidays festive. I pictured her as her own person, going about her own business, enjoying our common space. And I saw myself happy to have welcomed her in my house.

Without my having gone through steps one and two, I doubt we could have lasted together. I had to come to terms with every potential negative I could think of. A strong-willed 80-year-old mother set in her ways does not become a bit player (in her mind) on anyone's stage, especially her son's. She was used to setting the rules in a household and having things her way. Over the years, we had our ups and downs — frankly, she more than I. They never lasted very long, but they were hurtful. They never shook my resolve to stay focused on the bigger picture of providing a secure, loving environment for her — in spite of the odds. But my ability to do so was the direct result of my having psyched myself for our life together.

Third, only after getting through two hoops on my own, did I bite the bullet and let my mother in on my plan. I knew where I was in the process, but to get into her head and convince her, I needed a strategy. After all, she was the one who would appear to be giving up her independence, not by choice but by necessity. I had to find a way to preserve her dignity. I couldn't say I was concerned about her long-term health and well-being and wanted to take care of her. She would never have gone along with that; she was in great shape for a woman her age. Instead, I framed her moving in with me as a business opportunity, a wise financial move for both of us. With that story, she could save face with family and friends. It was tailor-made to appeal to her psyche and spirit of financial adventure.

In the plan I shared with her, moving in with me was simply step one in a two-step strategy. I suggested she sell her condo and join me, in advance of our buying an apartment building. I had it all figured out. She would live in one unit. I would be in an adjacent one connected to it, use a third unit for an office, and rent any remaining ones.

I was totally serious about my apartment strategy. I knew exactly which properties on which streets I would consider since I had long thought about buying one of them on my own. Aside from their investment potential, their great appeal was they looked like L-shaped ranch houses, not apartments, and were on residential, not commercial-looking, streets. I also knew how important curb appeal was to my mother: She would never live in a place which looked overly commercial.

Because mother was a hard-sell on any issue, I *always* had to lay the groundwork. Before she moved in, I took her to see the places I had in mind for us to buy. And once she moved in, we even drove by others to get her prior approval. The ones I really wanted were never for sale while we were looking, but we were under no pressure to move. In the meantime, my house was laid out so she had her wing and I had mine. We agreed we could wait for just the right property to come on the market.

Still, to prove that I was *really* serious, I contacted a real estate agent and we even visited some properties. But my mother nixed them all. I distinctly remember one place with a huge owner's apartment, big enough for both of us and with about four rental units. With a swimming pool in the middle, it was a smart piece of investment property. But she refused even to consider living there, objecting to all the unsightly parking spaces in the front — no matter all the tenants who would have been paying substantial rents would be parking their cars in them. Some things money can't buy, at least for some people.

Perhaps deep-down, mother suspected my apartment-buying proposal was an elaborate ruse, though it *really* wasn't, or she became content being where we were. We never bought an apartment building. But considering doing so served its purpose — and then some. Year after year, our odd living arrangement eventually settled into predictable patterns. We regularly went to a favorite Thai restaurant, where everyone made a fuss over her. I took her clothes-shopping when she seemed reluctant to drive or go out on her own.

Caregiving boils down to unshakable commitment. Even the most impossible things you may have to put up with become bearable once you commit. When in doubt, don't — until you're absolutely sure of the choice(s) you've made.

After all of my anticipation and planning, there's one positive thing I had no idea would come out of my mother's moving in: my total relief. It was as though a cloud I didn't know had been hanging over me had been lifted. I had no idea how much subconsciously I had been concerned about her well-being or the tension it caused. I used to call her multiple times a day to be sure she was fine. My anguish left me when she was with me.

There was no way I could have prepared for all of the specific things we went through in our 10-plus years together. The *only* way was to decide to go through them, no matter what or for how long — and to accept whatever came along. It turns out we dealt with a lot, but we handled it — only because we both took the time to put ourselves through the paces and get psyched for it.

The consequences of not committing wholeheartedly to caregiv-

ing can be catastrophic. It can literally be deadly to uproot older people from their surroundings and then neglect to fulfill promises made to
them. Caregiving may have a clear beginning, but it doesn't usually have
a predictable middle or end. You can only handle all the challenges in
between if you're absolutely committed to whatever might come
your way.

3

CONVERGING OF THE TWAIN

Let there be spaces in your togetherness.
– Khalil Gibran

Moving-in day was like a sit-com episode. On a Friday afternoon in 1998, my mother, endless boxes she had packed herself, along with choice furniture, arrived. My once-minimalist living room looked like a cross between a warehouse and a consignment shop. We had almost no room to walk. Nothing seemed to fit. When I actually saw my house in disarray, I must admit to being human enough to have asked myself what I had done to myself. But I was so sure of my decision, my self-doubt lasted no more than a nanosecond.

Day by day, my mother carefully and methodically unpacked, having meticulously numbered each of her boxes and inventoried its contents in a blue spiral-bound notebook. Miraculously, like the pieces of a well-crafted puzzle, everything came together in time. Her sofas fit where I had two chairs. Her silver, Wedgewood, and crystal filled once-empty spaces in my cabinets. With her prized Reed and Barton silver place-settings securely in place, we were on the way to becoming a household — of sorts, gradually.

Meshing our material possessions turned out to be the easy part. At first, my mother looked upon her role as definitive homemaker — self-appointed, of course. I never asked her to do anything. But you could hardly blame her for assuming any house where she lived would become her domain by default, no matter what she might have said about it's

Try to personalize your family member's place in your house to ease
the transition onto your turf. That said, no matter what I said or
did or offered to do, my mother always said she was living in my
house. Even when I told her it was ours, she never bought it. More
than once, I encouraged her to redecorate her room. She said no, but
I should have insisted. At the same time we merged our households
and lives, I now realize I should've bent over backwards to preserve
my mother's sense of her independent self by encouraging her to go
places and do things new to her on my side of town, in spite of her
rejecting all of my suggestions. That way, she would have felt less
like she was giving up anything by coming to live with me. And
she might have been more inclined to create a new life for herself,
instead of seeming simply to be living out her old one on my turf.

being mine. She took it upon herself to do the grocery shopping, which
she did twice a week, turning it into a social event, especially as her circle of friends grew smaller. An infectious people-person, she always returned from the supermarket flattered and amazed, commenting upon
how many people had spoken to *her*, completely oblivious of her role,
almost without fail, in initiating most, if not all, conversations.

Our period of emotional and role-play adjustment turned into the
episodes of a minor soap opera. A steady stream of mental nips and tucks
began. Two strong-willed adults don't suddenly occupy the same general
space after years of living apart, especially if they are mother and son.
A lovey-dovey script goes against all basic instincts. We struggled over
everything from psychological semantics to dinner time. When I said she
was acting too much like a mother, she told me I "would always be her
child." When I replied I would always be her *son*, but had outgrown being her *child*, I might just as well have been speaking Greek. She took of-
fense if I didn't like meals exactly as she served them. She interpreted my

saying I preferred one egg, not the two she served me, as a knife to the heart. Nor could she adjust to my not eating at appointed times, my having to go to dinner with a client at the last minute, or my not needing to have anyone cook for me at times — or at all, if need be. When we had guests, she took complete charge of all the preparations. I had no say, final or otherwise.

For the first six years we lived together, my mother was totally, remarkably, even overly, independent. Widowed in 1990 and in good health, she had been living on her own, even after she had open-heart surgery to replace her aortic valve and an artery to the heart. She dutifully kept her annual appointment with her cardiologist, but otherwise didn't need to go to doctors except for checkups and occasional minor problems. Shortly after she moved in, she had a painful sciatica flare-up, which she blamed on my tile floors. An obliging doctor put her in the hospital for a couple of days to save her any added pain from having to drag herself for tests from physician to physician. A couple of cortisone shots later she was temporarily on the road to recovery.

Well into her 80s, my mother was always the designated driver for her circle of friends, handled all of her financial affairs — balancing her checkbook down to the penny, never hesitating to question bank charges and arithmetic that didn't make sense to her, and typically being right. She took more care of me than I did of her. She *never* wanted anyone, or at least me, to do *anything* for her. Her mantra was "I can do it myself." Our lives together were parallel, intersecting at times and places convenient for both of us. We didn't get in each other's way.

A certain constitutional discontent never left my mother, however: It's what made her tick and why she always wanted to make things better. She insisted I redo the front of my house and put in a circular driveway. Like a dog with a bone, she never gave up once she was intent upon something. We made several excursions checking examples of various contractors' work. She rendered her verdicts instantly and without equivocation. Then, we made a project out of deciding what *we* wanted, which usually looked remarkably like what *she* wanted. And then, of course, there was overseeing the work once it began. Soon enough workmen discovered that the nice, smiling, little, old lady was watching their every move.

Mother's same constitutional discontent led her from time to time to regret ever having moved in with me. Occasionally, I'd come across a brochure from an assisted living facility in the trash or a newspaper with the classified ads for apartments circled. She'd even tell me she wanted to move back to New Haven, Connecticut, where she was born and lived until retiring to Florida.

Most of the time, she'd plot her escape on the sly. But now and then, she'd wistfully look at me and say, "What kind of a life do I have?" Of course, she nixed all of my ideas for getting her out and about: accepting invitations from potential new friends, visiting her few remaining friends, inviting friends in, going to the theatre, going to lunch or dinner, taking a trip to New Haven with me. I knew her negative reactions were either rhetorical, from the part of her fighting old age and decline, or ad hoc responses to something — usually my — irritating her. I never made an issue of them. And I certainly was never going to go along with her leaving. My answer to her was *always*, "You can't leave me. I need you." In response, she'd shake her head and flutter her eyes to suggest she was resigned to her fate, and answer, "I know." My trying to make her understand she was genuinely needed seemed to settle the issue and calm her — at least until the next time. The scenario never developed into anything even close to a possibility. For all I know, the whole routine was just a charade she fabricated to reassure herself she really was wanted and to remind me to appreciate her.

To a casual observer, the rhythm of our lives together — bouncing between highs and lows — might have appeared to be communal manic depression, if there is such a diagnosis, or a variation of *The Odd Couple*. But actually, both conditions would have been right, at some level. I got through it all by remembering the wisdom about human relationships in the line from Woody Allen's *Broadway Danny Rose:* "Acceptance, forgiveness, love." I accepted the good times (of which there was an overabundance), forgave the bad (of which there were many fewer), and embraced them all with love. That's at least as good a return-on-investment as any rational planning could have produced.

4

PASSING A CRASH COURSE
IN UNCONDITIONAL LOVE

A Jewish man with parents alive is a fifteen-year-old boy,
and will remain a fifteen-year-old boy until they die!
– Philip Roth

Successful caregiving begins and ends with unconditional love. And
unconditional love begins and ends with literally putting yourself
in someone else's skin. And that isn't just verbal mush: It's the
result of the definitive life-lesson a gut-wrenching experience taught
me almost immediately after my mother moved in. And as awful
as it seemed at the time, it saved both of us years of anguish and
transformed our relationship into a workable one. Most important,
it made it possible for me to become her caregiver in later years,
without a moment's resistance or regret. If it had never happened,
our lives together could easily have become intolerable.

At 79, when my mother moved in with me, she was still very strong, fiercely independent, able to do everything for herself, and even for me. At that time, I wasn't her caregiver in any way, shape or form. I was simply her adult son, with whom she *happened* to be living. She was tough, not in a brash, bullying way. But she had definite ideas about how things — make that everything — should be done, especially around the house: Her way. From where and how the garbage should be placed to when dish towels should be dried, it was her way or the highway. And she *always* stood her ground. Had she been a government, she would have been executive, legislative, and judicial branches rolled into one. No decisions would have been subject to appeal.

After decades of watching my mother operate, I admit she had an uncanny, intuitive way of *always* coming up with the right answer for *everything*, though, at any given time, I may have resisted accepting it. I inherited her strong-willed genes, along with a whole batch of an equally effective, but more passively resisting, share from my father.

An objective observer looking at the two of us might easily have concluded our living arrangement was destined to be feisty, at best — at worst, a clash of the titans. But the earth moved and the ground shifted on an otherwise innocuous evening at the theatre, when I got the biggest life-lesson I could ever have imagined.

Weeks of nips and tucks came to a head at intermission, when we went outside. I wound up standing with my back towards a steep staircase which led to the street. Though I was relatively far from it, my mother cautioned me, "Be careful or you'll fall." Above a whisper, I snapped back, telling her I wasn't a child and I didn't need her to look after me.

Instantly, she went mum, mortified as much by my outburst as the likelihood people nearby heard it. (My stomach still turns when I recount the incident — even after more than 13 years and all the good it produced.) Obviously, my overreaction

You have to tame your ego if you want to be a compassionate caregiver. My life changed, and I unwittingly prepared myself for the challenges of my eventual, round-the-clock role as my mother's caregiver. In a flash, my ego took a permanent backseat to creating a nurturing environment for my mother. Pure emotion, not an act of will, transformed my life, and not just as a caregiver but as a caring human being.

was triggered by all the pent-up, unspoken frustrations of our early weeks together, no doubt with a measure of unresolved lifetime issues thrown in for bad measure.

Sylvia K. Goldstein was always the master of the silent treatment: But after my outburst she went into overload. We didn't speak again until the drive home, when I broke the ice. Apologizing, I explained I had taken care of myself for so long, I wasn't used to being watched over. Emotionally, she replied, "You're all I've got. I just couldn't bear to have anything happen to you."

I wasn't the only "thing" my mother had. My brother cared about her as much as I did. But that's not the point. For the first time, I understood she now saw herself as depending completely upon me. She had given up her independent life to live on my turf. It never occurred to me to tell her I would never ask her to leave, because I considered it a given. Suddenly, I realized how deeply my words could wound her. Probably, in the back of her mind, she was insecure — afraid of offending me, afraid I'd kick her out. At that moment, I told myself nothing she could ever say or do was worth my destabilizing her — absolutely nothing.

Meditate on the wisdom in Samuel Goldwyn's dyslexic aphorism: "It rolls off my back like a duck."

I decided then and there to let nothing my mother said or did plug me in. I made a life out of liberating myself from what could otherwise have been a back-breaking raft of ducks. Frankly, if my eyes had not been opened as early as they were, I don't know how the scenario of my mother's moving in with me might have evolved — make that devolved. Of course, it wasn't always sweetness and light. We're human — and different. She liked Lipton; I liked green tea. She preferred a Teflon skillet; I'd rather cook with tempered glass. I overcame the hurt when, in melancholy moments, my mother said moving in with me was the worst thing she ever did. She was never regretful for very long — or at all in the last years of her life.

Over the years, I've read and heard a lot about unconditional love. Haven't we all? It's supposed to be the open-sesame of all real relationships, not just with parents. But frankly, I thought it was just hooey. I never could raise my consciousness sufficiently high to accept anyone else for who they were without my fine-tuning. And I never hesitated to suggest strategic adjustments to improve others, whether they asked for it or not. On the self-satisfied, flip side, I could never imagine adapting the perfection of me, myself, and I to accommodate anyone else.

Bottom line, no matter how I might have chafed at my mother's "suggestions" for my self-improvement, they were always expressions of her unconditional love. Once she moved in with me, I got to return the favor. I started by learning to bite my tongue — and really didn't need to progress much further.

5

DISCOVERING THE WISDOM OF ASKING, "SO WHAT?"

Nothing really matters,
Anyone can see,
Nothing really matters, nothing
really matters to me.
– Freddie Mercury

From a distance, my mother genuinely cared about all people — old, young; black, white; rich, poor — without strings. She melted at the sight of babies. Her heart went out to everyone. She had an overabundance of empathy genes, if there are such things. She recoiled at injustice, celebrated other people's successes and didn't have a jealous bone in her body.

My mother was also a caregiver before caregiving was cool. As my grandmother's only daughter, she had no choice but to devote a substantial part of her life to being available to her mother, especially after my grandfather died. My mother had a brother; but, as far as my grandmother was concerned, she was an only child. Though my mother usually played her role without complaint, it didn't always sit well with her. At times, she would half-jokingly invoke Somerset Maugham, labeling their relationship "of human bondage." She and my father didn't make their (I suspect) long-planned move to Florida until after my grandmother died and they finally felt free to do so.

My mother was also the primary caregiver to my father. In 1965, he landed in the hospital with a condition at first undiagnosed but wrongly assumed to be life-threatening. It turned out to be pericarditis, an inflammation of the membrane around the heart. Though he lived for the next 25 years, his overall health and a variety of conditions became the focal point of my mother's life. He had lymphoma that went into remission, an arterial bypass in his leg, a recurrence of lymphoma, and the onset of Parkinson's. Through it all, she managed both their lives, and I never heard her openly or seriously complain about what she was going through. She played the hand she was dealt. I can still see her steadying him along the walk from their car into their condo.

But my mother's brand of caregiving had one undeniable characteristic — I would say flaw: The closer she got to directly caring for you, the more you had to give in to doing everything *her* way — what you ate, how you dressed, where you went — no exceptions. The price she exacted for devotedly being there for you precluded any negotiations or small talk about decisions affecting your life. It was *her* way or the proverbial highway in all cases.

When she first moved in with me, she typically began setting up her code of household conduct. Paper trash was never to be placed in a convenient, large receptacle in the kitchen where it might accumulate; instead, it was to be put into a small plastic bag in the laundry room and then immediately deposited in the outside garbage bin when it was full. Food and anything attractive to bugs was immediately wrapped in plastic and deposited in the outside bin. What we had for dinner was what *she* decided; menus were not negotiable. Such overbearing conduct did not bother me, because I had spent a lifetime dealing with it — accepting, rejecting, even flouting her preferences at will. Plus, truth be told, my mother had uncanny instincts; she was generally right. So, most of the time, I saw no reason to resist.

As my mother began to show early signs of dementia, I had to

There's more than one way to skin a cat. Forget all your pictures of the way things should be. Just get the job done. Don't try to impose your will or get bogged down in trivial matters. In the scheme of things, little or nothing really matters.

learn how to be flexible — to train myself to find alternative scenarios for getting things done without provoking a confrontation, always potentially just beneath the surface. It was one thing to deal with someone as hardnosed as she was when she was mentally competent — quite another, after she began to fail. She still had the same determination, but there was no way effectively to reason with her. After much anguish and frustration, I eventually figured out that the autocracy typical of my mother as caregiver would never work for me providing care for her. Even with dementia, she was as likely to insist on doing things her way as she had always been.

To give my mother the care she needed, I learned the hard way not to delude myself into believing I could organize her life for her as I thought it should go. My role was to accommodate her, not hers to accommodate me. When I wanted her to eat and what I wanted her to do didn't matter. Giving her the best care meant I had to satisfy or work around her perception of her wants and needs.

In the end, my litmus test for dealing with what could have turned into contentious situations was So what? So what if she doesn't eat now? So what if she doesn't want to change her dress because she just got a spot on it? So what if she doesn't want to take a walk and get a little exercise today? As long as what she was doing or not doing didn't hurt her, so what? I learned not to sweat the small stuff.

I would have saved myself many sleepless nights, if I had learned the wisdom of asking So what? long before I did. Restless and sleeping fitfully, my mother began wandering through the house during the night.

In some houses such excursions wouldn't have mattered. But I installed an extensive alarm system, including motion detectors everywhere. I added an extra keypad at the door of her room so she could shut the system off and move through the house at will. But unfortunately, she eventually couldn't remember to do it.

Night after night, just about as soon as I had fallen off to sleep, my mother would begin to make her move — turning on all the lights, tripping the motion detectors, and waking me up. As the pre-alarm warning began, I had to get up and, during the fifteen-second grace period, turn the system off before the alarm sounded and prompted a call from the security company.

After I had disarmed the system, I would always find my mother in the kitchen, where she would be shuffling about, oblivious of having tripped the alarm, perhaps reading the newspaper — more like trying to. Foolishly, until I learned better, I would coax her to come with me, shutting off all the lights in the house as we walked together back to her bedroom, where I would try to calm her and get her back to sleep.

But invariably, after I thought she was down for the night and I was back in bed, in short order, she would once again be on the prowl, the house would erupt in a blaze of light, she would trip the alarm system, and the ritual would begin again. Because she was so tiny, sometimes she would wind up in the kitchen having eluded the motion detectors. Once in a while, she would open a perimeter door, the full alarm would go off, and then the call and rigmarole from the security system would begin: Who are you and what's your pass code?

When I originally installed my alarm system, it was to protect my house and me from intruders. But with my mother increasingly showing signs of dementia, it turned into a monitoring system to help me keep track of her during the night. For that reason, I didn't even mind being awakened repeatedly, if it meant she wasn't straying outside or falling or

Of course, the other side of So what? is What's so. With the alarm system disarmed, I couldn't possibly have rested, knowing my mother could have opened any of several doors to the outside — and wandered away on her own. For her protection, I installed dead-bolt locks on all the perimeter doors so high she couldn't open them. The locks could only be secured from inside by someone who was with her. So, there was never any danger she could have been locked in, unable to get out in case of emergency.

hurting herself without my knowing it for hours.

Until I discovered what I should have known and done all along, in an average night, the same pattern could repeat itself three to five times within a couple of hours: lights on, alarm system tripped, trying to get mother back to bed, hoping to get some sleep.

Eventually, I wised up. I asked myself the question I should have been asking all along: So what? Does it *really* matter if the motion detectors aren't on? And when I concluded we wouldn't be in serious peril, I simply bypassed them each night when arming the overall system. Eventually, after mother had opened a perimeter door one time too many, I asked myself, So what if I turn the whole system off? — and did so.

Once I learned the wisdom of asking So what?, I became a more joyful caregiver and my mother was happier, which is all that mattered. At times, when I've guiltily wished I had learned the lesson sooner, I've reassured myself by saying So what? — and that simple question has taken a weight off my mind. What's so was, as always, my mother got to have things her way. And, since feeling in charge always made her happy, it was all I cared about, as long as I kept her safe.

6

ALWAYS FOLDING THE NAPKIN

*Remember this — that there is a proper dignity and proportion
to be observed in the performance of every act of life.*
– Marcus Aurelius Antoninus

*Everyone needs to know, follow, and second-guess the wishes of
someone in their care. At an obvious level, they need to make sure
all necessary documents — a living will, healthcare surrogate,
durable power of attorney — have been signed and are in a place
where they can be easily found. That's easy. The greater challenge is
picking up on and caring about a person's more subtle preferences,
especially priorities and sensitivities they may never have uttered.
It's the difference between caring and simply providing care.*

I made sure my mother received the best medical care, including round-the-clock, paid, professional care at home when she needed it. I saw to the nuts-and-bolts of caregiving to be sure she was fed and clothed properly. I did everything professionals told me to do and that I knew to do instinctively.

But what superseded all of those obvious things was something indefinable and, ultimately, more crucial than anything else: My job as caregiver was to preserve my mother's dignity—at all costs. If I owed her anything, that was it, because it meant more to her than anything else. I don't ever recall hearing her say the word, but dignity was her "ruling passion."

A compelling story my mother told me gave me the most important clues to what made her tick more than 40 years before I had any idea
I would become her caregiver. In the early 1960s, my mother's aunt, and
my great-aunt, Alice was dying of cancer. Near the end, she was in the
hospital. There was almost nothing physically left of her. She couldn't
see or hear. She was barely alive and seemed virtually unconscious. My
mother was in her room when a nurse came in to give her a sponge bath.
But my mother said, when the nurse tried to uncover her to wash her,
our aunt, who, even in her near-coma, felt defiled, summoned up all the
strength remaining in her devastated body and resisted, grabbing for
something to cover her nudity and blindly flailing at the nurse.

My mother said she should have told the nurse to stop and to respect her aunt's dying wish. More than once, I told her the nurse had to
do what she had to do. But my mother always felt guilty for not having
stopped her — and amazed her aunt's sense of personal dignity appeared
to survive beyond everything else.

Like our Aunt Alice, a fundamental and protective sense of dignity
ran in my mother's veins. Partly, I think it was a trait typical of Eastern
Europeans, which she observed in the conduct of her mother, Aunt Alice's sister. It has nothing to do with how much money or social status
people have. Certain people have a certain presence and carry themselves in an assured way — shoulders back, back arched. It's not a physical, aggressive, or self-centered bravado. Other people simply immediately "get" who they are and where they're coming from. I don't think it
can be learned. I suspect the trait was genetic at some level and definitely
not uniformly transmitted. Members of my mother's family had more or
less of it, and it seemed more characteristic of the women than the men.

Wherever it came from, however, my mother's sense of dignity
was unique and complex. She didn't have a haughty or condescend-
ing bone in her body. She was anything but standoffish or a snob. Still,

there was an indefinable something — a line she would never allow to be crossed. It determined the way she did, and reacted to, everything. Her sense of dignity was a mixture of personal pride and honoring social norms at the same time. Her pronouncements could be sweeping and appear arbitrary, like the conservative way she felt people should dress in public. They could also be targeted and biting, like her disgust at how she felt Kirk Douglas had lowered himself and his family by titling his autobiography, *The Ragman's Son*. But they all had their source in her demanding a level of respect for each and every person she would not allow to be lowered.

More than once, my mother's sense of dignity morphed into moral indignation when she perceived someone else was being demeaned. When I was in junior high school in Connecticut, my class went on a trip to Old Sturbridge Village in Massachusetts, and my mother came as a chaperone. Today, the website of OSV boasts it is "a 'must-see' destination to experience early New England life from 1790-1840." But what my mother saw, instead, was something she could never bear — a good old-fashioned example of Yankee bigotry towards a black student by one of the female guides. I don't recall what the woman specifically said or did, or whether my mother said something to her. All I clearly remember is her fury — and what generally caused it.

To put the incident in even more perspective, it occurred in about 1955, when racial prejudice was very much a fact even in the supposedly tolerant Northeast — and overtly recoiling from it was rare to say the least.

Knowing as much as I did about my mother's "ruling passion," I had no choice but to preserve her dignity at all costs. It was the touchstone for every decision I made — even when it came to setting the dinner table. Small and otherwise insignificant-seeming things mean everything in life. I don't remember the name of the movie, but it was about the Second World War, I think. In it, a British prisoner of war made up his mind he would shave his facial hair daily as a way of preserving his dignity and not giving in to his captors. Remembering his resolve, every time my mother sat down to eat, whether for a snack or a full meal, I made sure I *always* folded her napkin evenly and precisely. It was my way of saying, we're not just eating and I'm not just putting any old bit of food in front of you. I haven't given up on you because you don't seem to know where you are and I can't get through to you. You are still a human being and entitled to the utmost respect.

I maintained my mother's dignity by attending to things I could see. I did everything I could to be sure she was clean and well-kempt, even when managing such routine matters wasn't easy. Too often, she refused to change her clothes when she really needed to. In addition, when we were with anyone else and her condition or care was the topic of conversation, I never talked about her or treated her as though she weren't there, as though she had no say in choices affecting her life, as though she had become an object.

I also maintained her dignity by keeping my cool when something happened to embarrass her — and that wasn't easy. Sometimes, she would spill her drink while she was eating, even occasionally dropping her glass on the floor. I didn't care about the glass shattering. I worried about the damage to her ego — and her cutting herself. She would appear disgusted at herself for no longer being able to do something as simple as holding a glass, and the disappointed look on her face broke my heart. In similar instances, I always immediately reassured her that the accident wasn't her fault and the loss of a silly glass didn't matter. I'd lie and say I was planning to throw the offending object out anyway. I'd blame myself for the slipperiness of the glass, or say I had filled it too high. I would do and say anything not to make her feel bad or lose face.

When my mother was bedridden, but still very much alert, I emphatically told nurses to respect her privacy. But as careful as they were, whenever anyone tried to bathe or change her, she resisted more vehemently than our Aunt Alice even did. At times, I would try to divert her attention from the indignity of what was happening to her. Eventually, she'd calm down, as all of us assured her we were only doing what was absolutely necessary. But we knew always to expect, and respect, the fight for her personal privacy from the undisputed champion of dignity for all. And it was the ultimate challenge and proof of our knowing how to care for her.

7

CREATING MIRACLES

For us, there is only trying.
The rest is not our business.
– T.S. Eliot

The family caregiver's motto should be the words of Dr. Benjamin Spock: "Trust Yourself. You know more than you think you do."

A number of years ago, I spent the better part of two days with the noted pediatrician. When I got out of my car to say goodbye to him at the airport, he engulfed me in the enormous expanse of his arms. There was no escaping. He openly acknowledged he had suppressed outward shows of emotion for the better part of his life and he was making up for lost time.

Even with all the medical and other professional resources available to everyone caring for the elderly, much remains unknown about people's needs and wants as they grow old. Family caregivers need to feel legitimately empowered to follow their best instincts and common sense to supplement valuable professional care. They are on the front line, able to monitor day-to-day changes in their family member's condition. They need to refine their radar so they can knowledgeably describe symptoms and seek the help of professionals when necessary. Trying is half the battle — and may yield twice the success most of us would imagine. And that's a prescription from Dr. Spock!

My personal, general mantra has two parts: There's always a solution. You just have to find it. My personal, medical mantra does too: Seek the best medical help. And patient heal thyself. Accepting responsibility for my life and never giving up are big parts of my DNA, inherited from my parents, as well as from the examples they set. Both of them worked hard and persisted until they achieved their ends, which weren't complicated, extreme, exotic, or selfish — chief among them, providing for our family. Without regret, my mother always said no one ever gave them anything, as in monetary inheritance or preferential treatment. They never looked for the easy way out and always accepted responsibility for decisions in their lives.

When a bad business decision forced my parents to close a company they never should have opened, they paid off every penny they owed, even though my mother had to go to work to help do it. I learned I had been accepted as a freshman at Columbia in my father's hospital room. A self-employed businessman, he was undergoing tests, and doctors feared his condition might be fatal. Fortunately, it turned out not to be. But even when my parents faced such uncertainty and possible family devastation, they both assured me that I would be able to go to the only college I wanted to attend. It wasn't because they were so fabulously rich, but because they considered my brother's and my education their priorities — and made sure they could realize them, no matter what they had to do without.

My parents' solutions to problems were always pragmatic, down-to-earth, meat-and-potatoes ways of meeting challenges. And they didn't simply amount to having or finding the money for something; it was more a matter of doing the right and appropriate thing. They didn't *hope* things would turn out as they wished; they relied on common sense and *made* them happen — and certainly didn't expect miracles.

Naturally, when my time came to be a caregiver, I was already primed with my parents' examples for assuming full responsibility for the role. It wasn't easy. My mother was one tough cookie. Her independence and strong-mindedness were at once her strengths and weaknesses. In some ways, she was her own worst enemy. She made my, or anyone's, trying to help her, very trying.

My first challenge was getting her to accept the idea I had any business presuming to offer her advice, let alone a role to play in helping her make decisions. She had always been a decision-maker and gave me remarkably good advice. As far as she was concerned, she had no reason to believe that anything had changed. Initially, she typically rebuffed my suggestions with a curt and emphatic, "I've been doing it this way all my life, so I don't need you to tell me what to do." Case closed — but not for long!

Shortly after moving in, she did need my help, though it took her a while to accept the obvious. Suddenly, mother experienced a debilitating, dagger-like pain down the lower left side of her body. She blamed what turned out to be sciatica on the tile floors in my house — naturally! In fact, it was surely caused by her having packed and lifted countless boxes as she prepared to leave her apartment — because she would *never* let me help her. I knew her tile-blaming was just her having buyer's remorse so soon after having moved in with me, and I let her complaints roll off my back—but I couldn't ignore the pain she clearly suffered.

In spite of the odds against me, I *had* to try and hope I could do her some good. To the amazement of oriental carpet lovers who visited us, I immediately put a Bokara in front of the sink in the kitchen to cushion the offending hardness she perceived in the tile, but it did no good. After numerous unsuccessful applications of Ben-Gay, mother agreed to go to our family physician — in a wheelchair because she could barely walk. We also went to an arthritis specialist to test her bone density, which we were delighted to learn she passed with flying colors. When cortisone shots didn't permanently relieve her pain, I suggested we go to an acupuncturist.

Initially, the mere mention of trying oriental medicine almost caused World War Three in our household. A traditional, hard-nosed, octogenarian, Jewish mother like mine doesn't do anything even remotely sounding off-beat before first dismissing it as ridiculous and out-of-the-question — especially when her son is the proponent of the *mishegoss* (Yiddish for craziness). But, after much begging and pleading, she eventually let me schedule an appointment, only because she was in so much pain — and because I imagine she felt my nagging and persistence were adding to her misery.

At the acupuncturist's, she rolled her eyes at the waterfall in the outer office and the New Age music being piped in. Her facial expression, which only I could interpret, betrayed total disbelief, as she listened to the especially solicitous doctor's proudly proclaiming his credentials from a medical school in China. I'm sure she had absolutely no idea what he was talking about when he began to describe the meridians, pressure points, and needles he'd be using to relieve her pain — or she would have bolted then and there. I'll never forget seeing her stretched out on her stomach with needles at strategic points in her body and darting glances at me, translated into words that would have ranged from "How could you do this to me?" to "I'll get even with you."

After the first of what were supposed to be multiple treatments — paid for out-of-pocket, which automatically doomed them in her Depression-era consciousness — we left with a small but pricey quantity of Chinese herbs, which she said she would take over her "dead body" — or did she mean mine? During the drive home she vowed never to go back. But when we got home, for the first time in a couple of weeks, she slept soundly for several hours and awoke without any pain.

The doctor suggested she begin a regimen of physical therapy by walking backwards to free up certain muscles, which I did with her. (Just imagine the two of us walking backwards down a hall for about 10 or 15 minutes!) In my evil imagination, I pictured her only relief coming from walking backwards for the rest of her life — and me there walking backwards with her! No surprise: We only did the whole regimen once or twice. Eventually, she valued her visit to the acupuncturist and forgave me for taking her. Finally, her pain went away, even though my floors remained tiled. The Bokara must have been at least part magic carpet after all!

Arranging for an older person's medical attention is obviously critical. But sometimes it may be an ordeal even to keep a doctor's appointment. It became harder and harder for me to get my mother to leave the house. And even when she agreed to see a doctor, she would often tell me to cancel at the last minute. Family caregivers can only do so much. If it becomes hard or impossible for you to bring your family member to a doctor, it is absolutely crucial for you to arrange for a qualified medical professional to come into your home regularly to assess her physical condition or treat him.

I tried to keep my mother active by taking her clothes-shopping when she seemed reluctant to go out on her own. I offered to take her to see friends and welcomed her inviting them to visit us. But, because fewer and fewer of them were alive and healthy, she gradually lost interest in socializing and kept more and more to herself. I think the watershed in her life came after she had an emergency appendectomy. She forever lost what remained of her lifelong spunk.

My mother always received the medical attention she needed. Her only prescription was for blood pressure medication. But I never trusted her to take it without watching to be sure she not only put it in her mouth, but actually swallowed it. I tried every common sense home remedy I thought might restore her strength and fading memory and bring her back to me — Ben-Gay, Aloe vera juice, glucosamine, vitamins, protein drinks, walking with her for exercise. She wore cushioned sneakers to make it easier to walk on my tile floors. She could regularly have exercised in the indoor swimming pool in my house. But she told me I was crazy to think she would go in it because it was too cold, though it was heated. More than once, I was tempted to pick her up and put her in, but I knew it would traumatize her. More than anything, I think a warm, loving hand applying soothing ointment to a frail, old body provided the psychological comfort that produced physical relief, real or imagined. Right after I'd put Ben-Gay on her aching shoulder, she'd always tell me how much better she felt. If only it lasted!

I noticed mother's hearing was failing, especially in her left ear, and wondered if something as simple as an accumulation of ear wax might have been responsible for some of (what we assumed were) her symptoms of dementia. Eventually, I found an audiologist who was licensed to remove ear wax and who was willing to make a house call. She took one look, said there was wax, but not enough to impair hearing, and accepted her check for $150, which I gladly handed over. No matter what the cost, I couldn't rest until I explored every option to improve her well-being.

Above and beyond anything I would do, I kept hoping against hope for a miracle — often enough, so I now understand why people go to Lourdes or believe in faith healers. If you truly care about someone, you will suspend disbelief and try anything to make them better, no matter how silly or crazy others think you are — or you may even look to yourself. After all, history is filled with examples of what are alleged to have been miracles. *Why not now and for us?* I asked myself. After all, in a whole lifetime, I was only requesting one miracle, and it wasn't for myself. It didn't strike me as pushing my luck.

In the end, I realized miracles are actually more common than I thought. They happen all around us and come in all sizes. Too often, we just don't recognize them. While I was trying and hoping for a big, undeniable, earth-shattering transformation capable of restoring my mother to her former state, I foolishly missed, right before my eyes, any number of smaller, more important, ones relieving her pain and keeping her smiling — and alive, in spite of the odds. Miracles happen inevitably, I came to understand, with help from a magic Bokara or two — as long as you keep trying to create them and heed Dr. Spock's advice.

8

KEEPING MY MOTHER FROM
CHOKING TO DEATH

. . . chance favors the prepared mind.
– Louis Pasteur

If you think you've ever experienced sheer terror from watching a horror movie, imagine watching as someone appears to be choking to death — and then, just imagine what I felt when it appeared to be happening to my mother *for real.*

A sunny Saturday started out as an ordinary, predictable, happy afternoon excursion. Though a family friend and politician had lost her election, she graciously invited all her supporters to a thank-you reception. My mother was in rare form, gregarious as ever. We met and greeted any number of friends and strangers. After helping ourselves to the generous buffet, we were seated next to each other at a table for eight, shooting the breeze with everyone.

Then all of a sudden, the terror of terrors struck. Mother gagged on her food, couldn't swallow, appeared unable to breathe, and grabbed her throat. I froze. For what seemed like an eternity, everyone at the table watched in horror. Fortunately, her anguish and our fright lasted only a couple of seconds. She threw up into her plate and napkin, breathed a sigh of relief, and insisted she was all right, though she was mortified and physically drained.

I was not all right, but in a state of shock. All I could think was I had watched her almost choke to death right before my eyes — but I absolutely, positively did not know what to do. It was all over so quickly, no one else had a chance to do anything like the Heimlich Maneuver — and luckily so. She was so frail, had anybody squeezed her with any amount of force, he would have cracked her ribs, or worse.

Learn how to handle choking incidents. They are not all the same. Most of us take swallowing, like breathing, for granted — until the unthinkable happens and something gets stuck in someone's throat and the person appears to be choking to death. Of course, at first, we panic, whether we're the victim or spectator. Don't take chances! Obviously, the first thing to do in what looks like a choking incident is to call 911. Then, while help is on its way, determine if giving the Heimlich Maneuver is appropriate because the person can't breathe. All caregivers should know how to do it. However, as long as someone can breathe through her nose and isn't turning blue, she's not in danger of choking to death. There are two pipes down there — one for food and one for air. If it turns out to be a swallowing, not a choking, incident, it's important for the patient to remain calm — and breathe. Eventually, what's stuck may pass; otherwise, medical attention may be needed to remove the blockage.

Mother recovered physically after her choking fright, but emotionally both of us were wrecks. The trauma lasted: From that day on, no meal was ever routine. I always prepared her food so it was easy to chew and swallow, watched what and how she ate, and was on alert to help her through many subsequent scary episodes, even though we came to understand that, because hers were the result of a swallowing problem, they weren't life-threatening.

After the first incident, when we got home and settled down a bit, I said I would make a doctor's appointment for her. But as usual, she said it wasn't necessary, she was over it, and everything was okay. Of course, I wouldn't give up, begging her to do it, if only for me, and she relented. Our family doctor diagnosed the problem as common: a narrowing of the esophagus from acid reflux. And he assured us, however horrible her condition may have appeared, she wouldn't have choked to death because she could still breathe through her nose. That's when I learned the first thing to tell her at the start of subsequent episodes: relax and breathe.

Eventually, a specialist confirmed the diagnosis, even showed us a picture of just how much her esophagus had narrowed, and performed the first of two procedures to stretch it. Before her first procedure, the doctor said mother should only eat soft food. Thinking *mother has to eat, it has to be soft food, or she might choke again,* in a panic, the only thing I could think of feeding her was baby food. I rushed out and bought a shopping-cart full of the stuff — broccoli, apple, chicken — anything looking as though it might appeal to adult taste buds. I couldn't let her see she was getting baby food or she would have gone ballistic. On the sly, I emptied a few jars on a plate and tried to make them look appetizing. I added seasoning. But no matter what I did, they were inedible. I wound up giving my sizable remaining inventory to a friend who had an infant granddaughter.

When I gave myself enough time to think of reasonable choices, I discovered a variety of sensible options — soup, potato soufflé, quiche, corn flakes, mashed up spaghetti, and fish (especially tilapia). But no matter what I served, I cautioned mother to take small bites, chew thoroughly, and eat slowly. I watched, holding my breath.

After the first procedure, the doctor prescribed a regimen of pills to cure the bacteria-caused ulcer he said had created mother's problem, but she couldn't tolerate it because it gave her diarrhea. No matter how many procedures mother had or what medication she might have taken, I was never going to be cooking-as-usual for her. The situation was complicated because, as she showed signs of dementia and her mental capacity diminished, I couldn't get her to understand what not to eat or how to eat to keep her from choking. I had to watch over her and remind her to take small bites, chew thoroughly, and eat slowly at every meal.

Bracing for what were sure to be repeated swallowing incidents, I began my trials and errors as a soft-foods cook. I learned soft is a relative term. For example, I knew steak was out of the question because my mother couldn't possibly chew it into bites she could swallow, but I discovered the hard way ground sirloin was no better. The smallest pieces of meat, if not properly chewed, could still clog the esophagus — and did. Mother loved eggs, but I only served them scrambled. Even the whites of sunny side up eggs could get stuck in her throat if she didn't chew them well enough. I had to make sure she ate the bagel she coveted every morning in tiny pieces — and then only the soft inside, not the hard, toasted crust. Spinach quiche was always a winner, because the grated cheese I used wouldn't congeal into a perilous lump.

I bought a Crock-pot, thinking I could slow-cook chicken to swallowable softness, but it didn't work. Even if it had, it wouldn't have

Preparing food for someone who has trouble swallowing doesn't need to mean serving mush, unless someone has no teeth and can't chew. And yet, when my mother was in the hospital and briefly in a rehab facility, meals routinely consisted of a helping of whipped brown meat of some variety, whipped green veggies, and a whipped potato or other carbohydrate. Nutritionally, such slop was balanced across all traditional food categories, but that's about all you could say for it. It was less than unappetizing. But anyone who can cook can cook "gourmet soft." Meals may be surprisingly simple and delicious to prepare — and healthful.

Once I exhausted my own list of likely ingredients and recipes, I went whole-hog and bought specialty cookbooks. I recommend two if your family member has trouble swallowing. The scary-sounding Dysphagia Cookbook: Great Tasting and Nutritious Recipes for People with Swallowing Difficulties *by Elaine Achilles does everything from showing you how we swallow our food to offering tips on preparing, serving and eating meals. Its recipes are as delicious as you'll find anywhere. The more homey-sounding,* Easy-to-Swallow, Easy-to-Chew Cookbook *by Donna L. Weihofen offers advice on posture and position during meals, acid reflux, oral hygiene, avoiding choking, and a number of related subjects, as well as more than 150 recipes anyone would want to eat. I served purees, of course.*

mattered, in her inimitable way, my mother made a blanket announcement she suddenly didn't eat "this kind of food" — a stew I had taken great pains to prepare with endless nutritious ingredients. Whenever possible, I got her to drink high-protein drinks in moderation; otherwise they might cause diarrhea. As time went on mother's eating was complicated by lost and loose teeth inhibiting her chewing.

For certain, though unpredictably, no matter what or how my mother ate, from time to time, she would choke on her food. Together, we learned what to do — especially not to panic. Eventually, it happened so many times she handled it better than I did. I never got over the horror of seeing someone appearing to choke, fearing this time it might be happening for real. Like everything in caregiving, you learn to live with a long list of things you never thought could happen — until the next one and the next one, and you somehow get through them.

Nutrition is crucial for the well-being of seniors. But there are so many variables, it's challenging to find healthful and savory recipes, since most family members are likely to have dietary and physical restrictions. The first rule to follow is: Don't serve anything to someone under your care you wouldn't eat yourself. There's always a way to make even the most restrictive diet palatable. Mealtime should be as festive as possible, a celebration for caregivers and their family member. In addition, as you watch salt and sugar intake and cook for easy digestion, you can serve your whole family healthful meals and educate them to eat well, no matter how old they are.

Once burned by the terror of a choking incident, twice shy of ever eating poorly — at any age.

9

BECOMING A NOBODY
WITHOUT A NAME

How dreary to be somebody!
How public, like a frog
To tell your name the livelong day
To an admiring bog!
– Emily Dickinson

The signs of my mother's dementia came on slowly enough for me to be able to avoid facing them — and save face for her — at least until the sad reality was undeniable. Once, on one of our trips to the doctor, a nurse sensed her disorientation and began firing questions at her: "What day is it today, Sylvia?" "Who's that man over there?" and similar insensitive assaults on her then-clouded intelligence.

In "her day," my mother could have run circles around the young woman. But in those few minutes, she was sadly flummoxed. Diplomatically, I suggested the nurse stop her barrage of questions. I'm sure she thought she was taking notes the doctor would have valued for her ongoing assessment of my mother's overall condition. But I couldn't let it continue. I had seen signs of my mother's confusion for weeks, but I pretended to myself mother's bewilderment could have stemmed from any number of things, though I couldn't have said what. This was the first time her condition was exposed beyond the safe confines of our home, and in a doctor's office no less. I needed time to adjust to the shock of reality slowly but surely creeping in. But my self-delusion wouldn't last long.

I became my mother's caregiver *for real* the day I realized she no longer knew my name. Until then, in her late 80's, she had simply been gradually showing the expected signs of her advanced age, from chronic aches and pains to the mild forgetfulness exhibited in the doctor's office — nothing severe. But one devastating day for me everything changed.

The first time my mother appeared not to know me, I didn't believe it. How could I? I thought her failure to recognize me was another example of her dry sense of humor and she was just playing with me. I host television programs, which my mother always watched — never hesitating to offer suggestions about how I should shake hands with guests at the end of a segment, how I should be dressed, and how and whether I should move my hands.

But one day, I walked into her room while she happened to be watching my newest show. "How do you like my latest interview?" I asked her. "That's not you," she said. "He's old, pointing to me on the screen." I replied, "Of course, it's me." She emphatically repeated that the man on TV wasn't me. I dropped the subject — confused and worried, to say the least, hoping I hadn't really heard what I clearly had.

The second time it happened, I died inside. I also write newspaper columns, and I always save the printed copy. One day, I showed my mother the day's column as I was folding the paper before filing it. She grabbed it and wouldn't let go. "You can't have that. I have to give it to Stephen," she insisted. She relented when I told her I wanted to read it and promised I'd give it back to her for Stephen.

The mother who had taken great pains to name me at birth eventually recognized me only as the primary, but nameless, person who cared for her. She would always tell anyone around her, "I love this man." But her clear expression of such deep appreciation was little consolation for me. She would sometimes refer to me as her brother or her uncle or call me Harry, my father's name. In a couple of eerie, isolated instances, out-of-the-blue she called me Stephen, in the familiar voice I had taken for granted all my life. *I have her back; she's come out of it,* I thought to myself, hoping against hope. But the recognition was momentary. Only my sad pain of unthinkable loss survived.

My world changed completely. From then on, I knew I would have to orchestrate her life — and my life around doing so. The reality of my mother's condition was undeniable, but I didn't have a clue about where it was taking us or how we might wind up. I knew for sure, though, we had crossed a line. Together, from then on, we would be living in a twilight zone. I was no longer simply a son whose mother was living with him. I had become a full-fledged caregiver.

For my mother's safety, I knew I would have to watch for signs of increased physical and mental deterioration. Beyond that, I didn't know what to expect. I panicked. I was terrified at the prospect of how bad it could get. Most of all, I was afraid a day might come when I myself wouldn't be able to care for her at home or hire enough people to do so.

Sadly, day by day, I watched her struggle to complete the cross-word puzzles or word scrambles she used to breeze through in ink. She could no longer read and know what she was reading. I could no longer trust her descriptions of pains and other medical symptoms, her answers to questions, responses to situations, anything she said or did. More and more, I knew I would have to think like and for her, and second-guess her. Worst of all, I saw her slowly slip farther and farther away from me, while I was powerless to do anything about it.

As time went on, I felt as though I were living in two, irreconcilable, parallel universes. The wishful half of my consciousness struggled to treat my mother as though she were the same strong, elegant, together person she always had been. In my mind's eye I remembered pictures of her I had seen — on horseback as a child, at home with my grandmother, with my father on their honeymoon. I saw her driving my brother and me and a car full of friends and relatives to the beach, as she did most days every summer when I was growing up. She was always at the center of things and always drew others in. She radiated warmth and caring like no one else. I replayed her central image in a phantasmagoria of countless images, all of them testifying to her unifying strength and exuberance, now forever lost.

In spite of seeing my mother obviously fading, the Superman part of me always hoped I'd find the vitamin, power drink, or psychological home remedy to snap her out of the fog into which she appeared to be retreating. And it wasn't just passing self-delusion on my part. Throughout my life, I honestly believed I should never assume the worst, give up hope, or stop experimenting and trying. After all, I asked myself, who *really* knows how the mind works? I remembered too many examples of people who had awakened from comas after many years ever to give up entirely on the possibility my mother

In all of my devastation and disbelief over my mother's not knowing me, one thought got me, and can get other caregivers, through it: My mother's not knowing my name or knowing me by name didn't matter. She knew I cared for and loved her. Infants don't know the name of the loving parent who cares for them, but they know instinctively when they're being fed, clothed, kept warm — all the good stuff. My ego had been shocked and bruised, but I learned my ego was totally unimportant. My mother recognized me as the person who was there for her — and that's all that mattered.
In the end, I learned the ultimate irony: I made a greater difference in my mother's life when I was anonymous than I did when she knew my name. And that, Emily Dickinson would have agreed, made it almost "dreary to be somebody."

would come back from wherever she was. But of course, the realistic half of me was coming to terms with the inescapable, stark fact of her being as diminished as she was, in front of me.

10

SCRAMBLING FICTITIOUS EGGS

The best liar is he who makes the smallest
amount of lying go the longest way . . .
— Samuel Butler

Thank God! In the most monumental change she ever orchestrated in her life, one day, my mother stopped driving, cold turkey, of her own accord. She never said why and wouldn't tell me when I probed a bit. I don't know if she got confused and lost her way or if she had a near-accident. All I know is, after driving for about 65 years, she never sat behind the wheel of her car again.

Of course, I was a bit sad, but mostly I was just totally relieved. I couldn't imagine her fury if I suggested she stop driving or if things became so bad I took away her keys. Consciously or unconsciously, all drivers associate driving with their independence. For my mother, driving defined her as an accomplished, self-reliant woman. She prided herself on being not just a good driver, but a *great* driver. In 1939, when she was 21, she got her license, at a time when few men, let alone women, did. And during the Second World War, when my father was away, she owned a car, when almost no one else did. In her eyes, Sylvia K. Goldstein was queen of the road. So, her abdication was a major turning point in her life.

Until mother stopped driving, her daily ritual included shopping for food or clothes. She no longer visited friends. She never went far or was out for long, but at least she found a reason to shower, get dressed, make herself presentable — and get out of the house. At the same time she stopped driving, I noticed she seemed reluctant to go anywhere.

Immediately, my relief at her no longer driving was offset by my concern she would lose even the limited social interaction she had. My taking her out on short trips — to the drive-in teller at the bank, for example — seemed a way to compensate for it. Of course, she'd tell me she wasn't dressed properly, but I'd remind her she wouldn't have to get out of the car. She beamed when the teller at the bank made a fuss over her. With a little coaxing, she genuinely enjoyed the brief excursions.

Eventually, I decided, if brief trips were good, longer ones would be even better. Late afternoon seemed like a perfect time for both of us to end the day with a leisurely drive. At least a few times, it was. We lived in South Florida where driving down the beach is always a treat. Away we went! Mother seemed genuinely to enjoy getting out. I couldn't have been happier.

I've heard countless, heart-wrenching stories of sons and daughters having to take car keys away from their parents because they can no longer drive safely. It's like pronouncing a death sentence. But recently, I heard how one family avoided all the sturm and drang of a direct confrontation: A clever son simply removed the battery in his mother's car. She had to accept the fact that her car wasn't working and he promised to have someone look at it. But of course, he delayed and delayed. And eventually, she found other ways to get where she needed to go.

Everything changed for the worse one day, however. We returned from a drive and walked into the house in the late afternoon. But mother seemed out of sorts. She stood in the middle of the living room, looking helpless and more confused than I had ever seen her. She stared at me blankly and said, "I can't stay here. I have to go home." My heart sank. I answered plaintively the only way I then knew how: "But you *are* home. This *is* our home." My words meant nothing. Sad, agitated and confused, she kept repeating she had to go home. I didn't know what to do. But after about 20 useless minutes of trying to calm and reassure her, I told her we'd get in the car and "go home."

We drove to the condominium where she lived before moving in with me. I hoped seeing familiar sights might jar her memory so she could update herself into our current reality. I wish! She recognized nothing. But, after about an hour driving around, my strategy worked because it tired her out. When we returned home, she said she wanted to lie down and rest. When she awoke, she was fine. It had taken the better part of two hours to bring us back to some semblance of normal. But we had clearly crossed another line, almost as shattering as when I first realized my mother didn't know my name.

On that eventful day when, for the first time, mother voiced her homing instinct, we entered a cruel twilight zone, when she appeared physically "there," but was helpless to relate rationally to her surroundings and me. It was as though a fog enshrouded her. There's a name for her behavior: Sundowners Syndrome. I'm grateful to my brother for having identified and told me about it. As he explained, in the late afternoon and early evening, literally as the sun goes down, people with dementia, Alzheimer's, and related conditions may become especially disoriented.

My mother would have many instances of Sundowners, but I couldn't predict them. She could go for days without showing any signs; then, out of the blue, her mantra would begin. Most often, it would start at about 5 p.m., but sometimes it would occur as late as 8 p.m. A devoted mother and wife, she dug deep in her subconscious and always said she had to go home to prepare dinner and take care of her children and husband. She'd look at me seriously, wide-eyed, and explain she just *had* to go. I'd tell her how much I needed her, too. She'd nod, agreeing and

Sundowners Syndrome is a real condition, though its name sounds kooky and unscientific. It has been estimated to affect as much as 20 percent of people with Alzheimer's, dementia, and similar conditions. Its symptoms vary widely — mood changes, anger, crying, pacing, general restlessness, a wide range of confusions and fears. Many possible triggers have been advanced — diet, noise, changes in light — but definitive causes are unknown. Some medications may be helpful, as well as over-the-counter supplements. But because my mother was firmly against being medicated unless it was absolutely necessary, I chose to deal with her Sundowners by being with her, calming her, and talking her through it. It could be exhausting, but I felt I was respecting what I knew to be her wishes, which was always my paramount concern.

appearing to weigh the pros and cons of the two demands on her. Then, she'd still insist she simply had to leave.

My heart sank every time she started, but I was more concerned about her anxiety than my discomfort. Once mother's Sundowners was no longer isolated or occasional, I knew I had to do something for both our sakes. Thanks to an exchange I remembered in Woody Allen's *Annie Hall*, which I believe was "inspired" by Groucho Marx, I found a solution. Woody, as Alvy Singer, says, "This guy goes to a psychiatrist and says, 'Doc, uh, my brother's crazy; he thinks he's a chicken.' And, uh, the doctor says, 'Well, why don't you turn him in?' The guy says, 'I would, but I need the eggs.' Well, I guess that's pretty much now how I feel about relationships; y'know, they're totally irrational, and crazy, and absurd, and . . . but, uh, I guess we keep goin' through it because, uh, most of us . . . need the eggs."

At first, it was difficult for me. I know that in the normal, day-to-day world, other people tell white lies for any number of reasons all the time. The fact they are "white" is supposed to excuse them from serious

I realized I needed to find an imaginary hen to lay at least a dozen extra large eggs if I were going to be my mother's most effective caregiver: I had to learn how to create "necessary fictions" to counter her fears, imaginings, and uncertainties at sundown. That's when I became adept at spinning tales that made my life and my mother's not only tolerable but even enjoyable. It was the last thing I ever thought I'd do. But it worked.

payback on earth or in heaven. But no matter what the color, I've never been comfortable massaging the truth as I knew it, even slightly, even for purposes of self-preservation. I'm not a paragon of virtue; I just can't lie and get away with it. When I'm dissembling, you can read it on my face — as my parents could when I was a child. But, as the saying goes, "any port in a storm." I had to figure something out — and fast.

Whenever mother said she "had to go home," she would identify the people who needed her and whom she needed to see as "they" or "them." I would tell her "they" just called and said "they" absolutely loved her and wanted to see her, but because of a serious accident, traffic was backed up for miles, it was raining, the streets were flooding, and it was a "dark night."

Instinctively, I repeated "they" and "them," because I sensed I needed to use terms from her reality to match the fiction I was creating. In addition, to make sure she wouldn't feel rejected, I made sure I underscored how much "they" loved and absolutely wanted to see her. I carefully chose my arsenal of negatives to dissuade her from wanting to go out. They were a mega-dose of circumstances I knew my mother feared — accidents, traffic jams and dark nights. She would cite them as reasons for my not going out or for my needing to be especially careful if I were driving, especially when I first got my license as a teenager. I used to laugh and tell her all nights were dark. But she was right: Depending upon the moon, the night could be lighter or darker. Her "dark night" and other phobias came in handy decades later. I knew they would probably make her not want to leave — and I was right.

To end my story on a positive note, I added "they" said she should stay the night with me, and when the weather cleared and the road conditions improved, she could go home the next day. "Things are bound to improve in the morning," I'd add to reassure her. Calmly, as though she had *really* gotten the message and was grateful for it, she'd say, "Okay." And I'd reply with a rousing, cheerleaderish, "C'mon into the kitchen and we'll have a party, just you and me." She'd laugh, and away we'd go.

Elsewhere I've described other fictions — my convincing her I was a hairstylist to let me give her a trim or my saying I was a doctor to get her to take a pill she might temporarily refuse to swallow. Nothing equaled for breath and ingenuity my hazards of the road tale, however. It was my biggest challenge, and I lived in fear it might someday fail.

When mother's Sundowners first appeared, I almost felt Chicken Little was right to declare the sky was falling down. But in the end, my mother and I had all the eggs we needed — and then some. And that's the absolute truth — no lie.

11

ALWAYS SPEAKING TO THE PERSON WHO'S *STILL* THERE

It is only with the heart that one can see rightly;
what is essential is invisible to the eye.
– Antoine de Saint-Exupéry

From all outward appearances, people with dementia or Alzheimer's appear to be physically there and emotionally elsewhere — cut off from us, living completely or partly in their own world. It's the saddest thing for anyone who loves them to experience and accept.

The problem is: None of us knows how far gone they *really* are — or how in touch with us they may still be without being able to show it. For that reason, I *always* treated my mother as though she were the person she had always been. I never gave up on her or treated her like an object or lost cause. I wasn't living in denial about her condition; I just wasn't willing to write her off without unshakable proof that she was beyond my reach. And to be truthful, I doubt I would have given up even then.

In her prime, my mother was small, hovering around five feet tall and never heavy, curiously petite standing next to two sons six feet tall. She was self-conscious about her height and, with a puckish wink, always made herself out to be slightly taller than she was. She was living proof that *real* power has nothing to do with size. In fact, I would guess there's an inverse ratio: the smaller the mother, and the taller the sons, the more she develops her inner strength — at least it's how my mother compen-

I believe I have positive proof there's still someone reachable behind the veil seemingly separating us from people with dementia or Alzheimer's. My conclusion may not stand a test in a laboratory experiment, but it passes the test of experience — which trumps statistics, and which is all I need.

No matter how distant my mother appeared to be at any give time, I knew from her vice-like grasp of my hand she knew someone was there for her. That's why I made sure I showed I cared in physical ways, not just with words. I held her and kissed her. And even when she couldn't sensibly answer me or acknowledge my talking to her, she always let me know she knew me through her hands. It pained me to let go when I had to, because I never wanted her to think I was abandoning her. To reassure her, I always whispered in her ear "I'll be back," clasped and unclasped her hand several times as though signally an ending to our current time together, and made sure to clench our hands together again as soon as possible.

sated. Her iron will held our family together. After my father developed health problems, she catered to him for 29 years. She had a bottomless well of personal commitment and an abiding sense of responsibility. She was a rock. She *always* came through for her family and friends.

As a child, I remember seeing my mother in an evening gown, with long black gloves, her hair pulled back, beautifully coifed, on a night when she and my father were obviously going out to a formal affair. I even have a photo of her dressed liked that. I also see her in a chocolate brown, tailored, stylish, cloth coat, which she preferred to her furs. I picture her in endless caring moments — comforting me when I had a fever as a child, taking care of my grandmother, helping my father walk when he showed mild signs of Parkinson's. I remember her in her office in business, doing yeoman's work — at the same time running a household. She was tireless, funny, engaged, self-effacing.

But in her failing years, mother became a wisp of her former self. Physically, she compressed from being small and strong into tiny — and frail. Mentally, more and more, she lived mostly in her own, remote world, only occasionally connecting with me — and then, on her terms, not on reality's, at least as I knew it. We were gradually only able to communicate at a basic level, and then only if I initiated the conversation. I could tell her I had prepared a meal for her and get her to join me. But she would never say she was hungry or thirsty. Gone were the days when she would read, and delight in, my newspaper columns, the first to read them.

Even though my mother appeared to slip away, I always treated her as though she was the person she had always been: completely "with it." And I soon discovered, no matter how demented, uncommunicative, or otherwise remote she *appeared* to be, underneath her fuzzy exterior she was "there." She was *still* a person. She *still* had real feelings and genuine responses. I can't say how much of her knew precisely what was going on around her, but I *can* say she knew at some level. To my joy and amazement, every now and then, a glimmer of her former self would shine through. She'd call her mother's or father's name — or knowingly respond to it if I mentioned it. Of course, such moments of recognition never lasted, but they put me on guard, never to assume I had completely lost her — or she had lost touch with me. As out-of-place and disembodied as her words may have been, I took them as attempts at engagement from wherever she was in her mind.

When I invited guests in for dinner, on the off-chance she would eat with us, I always set a place for my mother, even when she no longer would, or could, join us. I know the empty place must have seemed a bit eerie to my guests, especially when we knew there was no way she would appear, but I just couldn't bring myself to exclude her. If she ever said yes, I didn't want her to have to stand by the table, feeling like an afterthought, awkwardly waiting to be included, when she had been the organizer and life of so many family dinners and parties for so many years. I wanted her to feel and know she *always* belonged, was expected and missed.

My mother was the quintessential "giving" person, not just the consummate mother. She lived to love and give of herself to others, not just her family. And even as she was failing she never lost her ability to express her love. Her face lit up when she saw a baby on TV. She didn't have a prejudiced bone in her body. And even as she was failing, if she saw a person of color on TV who had obviously succeeded in some profession or circumstance, she would say "That's good — for everyone." I knew *exactly* what she was saying.

Here's another reason why I think everyone should assume people who appear to be beyond our reach may well be aware of most, if not, everything—or at the very least more than we imagine. In the eeriest example I know, a daughter who put her mother in a nursing home went to visit one day. Suddenly, her mother, who had for months seemed to be completely "out of it," looked her straight in the eye and said, "You said you'd never put me in a nursing home"—and then fell back into her usual stupor. That's a horrible experience for anyone to have to live with—but a major lesson for everyone to learn.

12

TRYING TO GET THROUGH TO THE PERSON WHO ISN'T "THERE"

Any port in a storm
– John Cleland

There is nothing more devastating than trying to communicate with someone living and breathing in front of you, who looks normal from all appearances — but isn't. My mother's dementia didn't happen precipitously, like a broken bone. It came on slowly. The early signs — forgetfulness, irritation, anxiety — didn't automatically indicate anything serious; we all forget things from time to time and become irritable and anxious.

But as it became obvious her condition was deteriorating and *was* serious, trying to deal with her was not always sweetness and light; it was heart-wrenching, filled with frustration, even anguish — day by day, even minute by minute. The living, breathing part of my mother that *was* left, the person who *was* interacting with me and physically present, was often unpredictable, going from nice to nasty or the reverse, without provocation, in a flash. I could no longer reason or discuss anything with her. At times, I felt like a pin cushion, put on this earth to absorb slights and hurts while I was trying my best to keep her healthy and happy. Sometimes, all I could think was, *No good deed goes unpunished.* At other times, I didn't know what to think or do, or where to turn. In the end, by trial-and-error, I developed a series of different approaches to get through to her. People say "necessity is the mother of invention." But in my case, *mother* was the necessity *for* invention.

I watched as my mother, a woman who had been in business and who took pride in balancing her checkbook to the penny, could no longer write a check or sign her name. Going about even the simple tasks of daily liv-

One of my successful approaches to get through to my mother was: Let's do it together.

ing became a struggle. In the last two years of her life, without my coaxing or pleading, she wouldn't have eaten, changed her clothes, brushed her teeth, washed herself — done anything. She was physically capable of doing them, but mentally incapable of thinking to do so.

Of course, I couldn't just suggest my mother do something like comb her hair or brush her teeth — or, God help me, tell her! In her more lucid moments, she would become offended at my appearing to order her around; at other times, she would stare blankly, as if my words didn't register on her at all. Nor could I forcibly brush her teeth for her. So, I started doing things *with* her. Instead of telling her I thought she should brush after we ate, I told her I was going to do so and suggested we brush together. "Come on," I'd say, "let's take care of our teeth, you and me." I'd get my toothbrush and the two of us would march into her bathroom and play the game of "the family that brushes together." In those moments of playful enthusiasm, I'd also get her to let me check to be sure her gums looked healthy. I used the same tactic for helping her pay her bills, few as they were. Our doing things together took the potential sting out of

my appearing to her to be trying to run her life — which is precisely what I was doing, of course.

Not *what* I said but how I *began* saying it determined whether mother's

Another useful approach was: The warm up.

response would likely be positive or negative. In other words, my challenge was to *sell* her on everything, especially the basics — like eating. For example, if I simply told her dinner was ready, I left myself open to her saying she couldn't possibly eat what I made. She would walk into the kitchen, but no matter what I had prepared, her first response would be she thought it was awful — and she'd turn around in disgust and walk out. By starting off as a cheerleader, on an upbeat note, I discovered I could more easily get her to do what was good for her. Usually, my strategy began in her bedroom. I'd tell her I prepared something special for both of us and I was so happy we would be eating together. I'd tell her how pretty she looked. I'd walk with her, hand in hand, to the kitchen. Then, I'd make a big deal over the food. Most of the time, it worked.

Yet another approach I used to get through to her was: The Impersonation.

To get her to let me do things she ordinarily wouldn't allow me to do, I tried to convince her I had professional credentials to help her with everything from personal grooming to pain relief. My mother was not vain, but she was always impeccably dressed and always had her hair "done." After a while, because she refused to go out of the house, going to a hairstylist was out of the question. Getting someone to come in wasn't practical either, because I couldn't be sure she would let a stranger near her.

I needed a ruse, because it was especially difficult for me to see her let herself go. I couldn't stand it when her hair grew long and she looked unkempt. At first, I suggested I cut her hair, but she looked at me as though I were crazy and refused to let me do it. Then, I wised up: I told her I was a cosmetologist, I had gone to school to be a hairstylist — and I would cut her hair for free, always a surefire selling point with any post-Depression-era parent. My mother may have been "out of it," but she wasn't stupid. She looked at me quizzically, but eventually gave in — especially after I kept insisting upon my stellar credentials and reminded her I was cutting her hair for free. Though I knew absolutely nothing about cutting hair, I did an acceptable job of trimming and shaping hers, especially since no one would see it.

Key to my success was involving her in the process. She would be in front of the mirror, carefully monitoring my every move, guiding me — and I kept asking her if I was doing okay. The end result was infinitely better than I ever expected. At least she didn't look shaggy and unkempt. In fact, with the last trim I gave her I thought I had outdone myself. I even started believing I *was* a cosmetologist.

My mother was stoic; her first instinct was never to complain. In 2003, she had an emergency appendectomy. Camouflaging her pain until it had become excruciating, she was doubled over, and her condition almost became toxic. At all times, I had to be especially vigilant to see if she was in pain she wouldn't admit to. Even then, if I offered to help her, her first inclination was to say she was okay. Adding to my self-professed credentials, I told her I was a doctor. If her frail bones ached, I'd rub Ben-Gay on the affected area — always telling her I had gone to medical school, if she resisted, and I would make her feel better. I never started believing I *was* a doctor, however. I knew where to draw the line. But I did *actually* relieve her pain.

After my mother had (what appeared to be) a slight stroke, she was in a rehab facility. Fortunately, I was able to go there four or five times a day, because it was near my house, generally

My almost sure-fire formula for getting through was: "Do you love me?"

arriving about 20 minutes after meals were served. I wanted to make sure, if she was inclined to eat on her own, I wouldn't be making her dependent upon me. But if, as was often the case, she hadn't been eating very much, or was refusing to eat, I saw to it she did. (I even left a homemade quiche with the staff so they could offer it to her if I couldn't get there and she refused to eat one of their meals.)

That's when I discovered the magic formula to get through to her: four little words, "Do you love me?" The process began with my kissing her, telling her how wonderful she looked and how delicious the meal was. (It wasn't, of course. Because my mother had difficulty swallowing, her food was pureed, and the menu never varied. But at least it was nutritious.) Then, my strategy devolved into pure histrionics that would have put Sarah Bernhardt to shame. "Do you love me?," I would ask. "Yes," she would always answer. "Then, please just eat this," I would say as I fed her. It worked every time. During a single session, I had to keep going through the routine of asking her if she loved me countless times to get her to finish a meal, but I didn't care. (There was poetic justice, karma, in my having had to go through such machinations to get my mother to eat: I was a picky eater growing up. I think I overreacted to her trying to shovel food into me when I was an infant and toddler. Now, I was paying the price when the tables were turned.)

Unconditional love is the way to get through to the person who isn't "there."

I also learned to deal with my mother's resistance and negativity by saying to myself, *She would never want to be in this state; but if anyone else were, she would give them all the love and understanding she could find.* Again and again, I learned the power of the patience springing from infinite, unconditional love. It's the open sesame almost certain to get through to the person who isn't "there."

13

DEMANDING MY MOTHER'S DUE—
AND GETTING IT

Pray for the dead and
fight like hell for the living.
– Mother Jones

My mother's well-being was my *only* concern. I took my role as her advocate very seriously. I wasn't obnoxious about it, but a major part of my role as caregiver was to see to it others upheld their part of the bargain when she was in their care. And if I hadn't, for sure, they wouldn't have. Sadly, the world is a hostile or indifferent place for people who are frail and elderly. Too often, people, even professionals, who should care, and who are being paid to care, think because old people appear to have one foot in the grave, they shouldn't bother trying to get it out.

Like all adults, my mother had a unique personal history. Because of her lifetime of experiences and choices, I knew her inner strength. I knew if anyone could muster the will to live, she could. And yet, no doctor or health professional ever took a "caring" medical history of her — asked her, when she still possessed her faculties, if she exercised or what she ate, or asked me to describe her, when she could no longer describe her lifestyle herself.

No one ever thought to get me to talk about my mother as a person to find out if something, beyond what might have shown up in a test, might have affected how she would tolerate a procedure. I volunteered she was living with me, but no one ever asked how she was being cared for in any detail. Instead, we just filled out the same forms every doctor wants, listing her few previous conditions and her negligible prescriptions. They were only interested in numbers — her cholesterol level and her blood pressure. I gave anecdotal information about how she was living and being treated, where and when it seemed appropriate. But if I hadn't, no one would have filled in those blanks.

One time, when it really counted, I intervened with a piece of information about my mother everyone else had overlooked, including the doctor. Had I not done so, the consequences could have been catastrophic for her — and him. She was going to have a routine procedure to stretch her esophagus because she had trouble swallowing caused by acid reflux. The doctor didn't remember her aortic value had been replaced, even though it was clearly indicated on her medical history. But I reminded him, adding that I couldn't agree to the procedure until her cardiologist checked her valve. I didn't want her to have a stroke or die because her valve wasn't working properly enough for her to undergo the procedure. It turned out everything was fine. But it might not have been.

If I could do it over again, I would write a profile of my mother and hand it to doctors as part of her medical record. The typical boilerplate medical work-up and patient history is the same, a tiresome list of past ailments and treatments and current medications you have to fill out over and over again. But a key factor in people's health and well-being is who they are as a person. Wise caregivers should take the initiative and surprise doctors by providing a profile — and going over it with them.

I know there are many fine and dedicated medical professionals. But once my mother showed signs of dementia, that condition and her advanced age seemed to justify too many of them treating her as a lost cause. As well-meaning as they may be, with so many people living longer and longer, I honestly think they just don't know how to deal with seniors, especially the oldest of the old. Some quote statistics. With blank looks on their faces they repeat assessments like: After age this or that, the percent of this or that will lead to this or that. Others can depress you with broad-brush, anecdotal diagnoses: Your mother's condition is only going to get worse, I was told more than once. Perhaps they thought hearing bad news helped me reconcile myself to my mother's inevitable decline and, at the same time, freed them from having to practice medicine — to put forth a serious effort to relieve pain and suffering and reverse decline, or just treat someone like a human being. I didn't care for any of it.

None of the collective "wisdom" of modern medicine persuaded me to sit back and do nothing. I wouldn't accept data and information that didn't appear to be applicable to my mother's condition or her ability to deal with it. That's not being pig-headed or living in denial; it's being totally realistic. I'm not the patron saint of lost causes; I simply come from the school of "Never give up on anyone until they are dead," because that's been the story of my life. I was never pushy or nasty about it, but I wouldn't be pushed around or allow my mother to be, either.

The last time my mother was in the hospital, it was because she appeared to have had a stroke, which left her barely able to stand and unable to walk. She also appeared more confused than usual. She went in on a Thursday. Saturday morning, I received a call from the hospital, telling me the doctor had released her and I could pick her up. I was elated. Because she was supposed to be getting physical therapy, I assumed she must be back on her feet. During the course of her brief stay, I had been told she had once been found in another patient's room. Though I was concerned about her having wandered away unattended, I took the report to mean things were looking good because she was strong enough to walk around.

I immediately went to the hospital, and happily announced to my mother that we were going home. But when I called the nurse to help her out of bed to get her dressed, she appeared to be in almost the same condition she was in when she was admitted. She was able to stand, but was unsteady — and she didn't appear to be able to walk on her own. I asked the nurse how she could possibly be released when she couldn't walk. "Hadn't she been given rehab?" I asked. "She's been exercising in bed," I was told. "Rehab in bed to improve her walking?" I asked in disbelief. "Please call the physical therapist," I insisted, my outraged look impossible to conceal.

When the physical therapist arrived, we again got my mother out of the bed so she could evaluate her condition for herself. "What's your assessment?" I asked. "She needs 24-hour care," she answered emphatically, and a bit embarrassed. "Thank you," I replied. Then, I asked the nurse to call the doctor and inform him my mother was in no condition to leave the hospital and he was to cancel her discharge order. (How's that for demanding her due?) I also asked her to tell the doctor I would appreciate his calling me so we could to discuss her continuing care. He told me there were two choices: She could come home and receive physical therapy two or three times a week, or she could go into a rehab facility for about three weeks and receive 24-hour care.

As devastating as it was for me to agree to my mother's going into rehab, especially after I saw the condition of other people there, I knew it was the best place for her. My brother and I had no intention of leaving her there for more than three weeks, the standard period of time for rehab. I chose a facility a few minutes from my house, where I knew the owner. I made sure he knew my mother was there, because I was confident he would tell the staff to treat her well. I visited multiple times a day, unannounced. I made sure everyone knew my mother was there strictly to get the most out of rehab, not to be warehoused. After a little more than three weeks, she came home — able to walk on her own, even having enjoyed her stay. We made the right decision — or, more accurately, demanded the right decision be made.

Once she came home, she continued to receive physical therapy. There were days she walked well and days she couldn't. I don't know what kind of statistic or anecdote her condition might have provided her doctors or medical science, nor do I care. She was number one on my list of priorities — and I demanded others treat her equally well.

A 2010 survey of 1,005 physicians reported 75 percent of them believe miracles can happen, a five percent increase in just two years. Fifty-three percent of the doctors surveyed said they pray for their patients, up from 49 percent in 2008. There was also an uptick in the percentage of physicians who reported they encourage their patients to pray because of its perceived benefits. To be sure, mental attitude in whatever form is critical to any patient's general well-being and healing. But I hope those doctors aren't praying because of what they know are the failures and limitations of modern medicine — or worse, their own inadequacies.

To other caregivers, my mantra is "Pray but advocate." I agree with Mother Jones. While others may be only praying, responsible caregivers have got to "fight like hell for the living" and assume no one else will — because they won't!

14

CHANGING MY MOTHER'S DIAPER

Just do it.
– Nike athletic shoes

More than once, I have written about the overwhelming joys of caregiving, unexpected moments of laughter and love. And I'm not about to take any of my observations back. But now, I owe it to any caregiver, or potential caregiver, to get right down to the nitty-gritty. There are things I had to do I could never have imagined. In fact, I still can't believe I had to do them.

The mother who had changed my diapers eventually was forced to succumb to the indignity of my changing hers, in the final weeks of her life. Even as I write this I anguish over saying anything about so private a matter, both for my mother's sake — and my own. She was the most private of people and, even in her debilitated condition, resisted everyone's — even female nurses' — attempts to bathe or change her. Part of me didn't want anyone ever to know what I had to do and remains skittish about it. But it goes a long way to explaining why I've written about my experiences as a caregiver: There are no holds barred. Caregivers need to know the truth about what they may be getting into so they can deal with it.

After my mother suffered what appeared to be a minor stroke, she became incontinent. When she returned home after being in the hospital and in a rehab facility, she was in a diaper. I had no idea of the extent of her incontinence. But I knew one thing: my having to change her was unthinkable, completely out-of-the-question, the absolute last thing in the world I would ever do. I always dreaded the possibility she would become incontinent, because I knew it would mean having to arrange for help to care for her in the most personal way, something she would vehemently resist.

With mother's return home, I arranged for Mrs. Helen Vinson, my housekeeper, to come five days a week, primarily to care for her. Because Helen once worked in a nursing home, she was a godsend. Mother came home on a Thursday. Everything was pretty much under control — until Saturday evening. Helen left at 4 p.m. At about 6 p.m., I discovered mother soiled herself, but there was no one but me to change her. With all of the planning I had done, I was still living in denial. I thought I could somehow continue to handle my mother's situation, even when just the two of us were together. I panicked. *I can't possibly change her,* I said to myself. But I knew I was only kidding myself. Staring me in the face was a little old lady who needed to get clean, fast—and I was the only one at the time who could do it. Looking away from her body, I told her I needed her to help me, and I began to remove the diaper. Resistant to anyone's invading her privacy, she physically pulled away and, thinking someone might rescue her from my evil clutches, immediately began yelling, "Help! Help! Hello! Hello!"

I don't know what possessed me, but hearing "Hello, Hello," I began singing "Hello, Dolly, yes, Hello Dolly, it's so nice to have you back where you belong." The absurdity of my spontaneous outburst caught mother off guard. She quieted down and stared at me in disbelief. I don't know where the energy or know-how came from, but, in a few short minutes, I whisked the diaper off her, cleaned her, and applied lotion to her so she wouldn't chafe. Because we used a panty diaper, at my plaintive urging, she even helped pull up the clean one. Miraculously, in the process, I never violated her privacy.

Helen didn't come on Sundays, but I got through the rest of the weekend on my own, thanks to several choruses of "Hello, Dolly." I knew things had to change — immediately. Monday, I arranged for round-the-clock care seven days a week. My strict instructions were my mother was never to be soiled for even a minute. On rare occasions, between shifts, when paid staff had not arrived, I continued to sing my heart out. But over time, changing her diaper became easier and easier. I learned to think like a son but to act like a clinician, to achieve the compassionate objectivity I needed to get the job done — because being up to doing the unthinkable, but necessary, is all that matters.

When I was arranging for round-the-clock care, I told the nurse taking our information how devastated I had been to have to change my mother's diaper. She looked at me and said, "Just do it. If you want to do what's best for your mother, forget everything you might think or have thought that would keep you from getting the job done — and act clinically. You are a caregiver first, her son second." From that moment on, I became the fastest diaper-changer in the Southeast.

15

GETTING USED TO FINDING A SANDWICH IN THE CLOTHES DRYER

And if I laugh at any mortal thing,
'Tis that I may not weep.
– George Gordon, Lord Byron

From Wonderland, Alice eventually awoke to discover her disquieting, unpredictable excursion was just a dream. For better or worse, the world again made sense to her. In my world, things were all-too real, but made less and less sense as time went on — and there was no prospect of waking up from, or avoiding, them. A topsy-turvy world just goes with the territory when you're living with a person who has dementia. I went from shaking my head in disbelief, wondering how this could be happening to me, to bracing myself for what strange scenario might be next. And no matter how used to our new reality I became, I was never able to predict what might occur — or when it would happen.

The one consistent fact of

When I suggest that laughter is really the best medicine for the stress and frustration of dealing with daily life with someone with dementia, of course I'm not talking about the belly-laughs delivered by stand-up comics. The kind of laughter I'm talking about is generally accompanied by shrugging your shoulders, shaking your head, raising your eyebrows, and perhaps releasing a sigh — all of them adding up to an unspoken "that's life!"

life for us was we were almost *always* looking for something. Of course, young and old, everyone misplaces things from time to time. What made us different was we were on a never-ending scavenger hunt. We were constantly turning over pillows, crouching under furniture, retracing steps, scratching our heads in pursuit of one thing or another. Almost guaranteed, daily, we'd be on the hunt for my mother's reading glasses, without fail if we happened to be going out to dinner. We'd both be dressed and ready to go, often meeting people at a designated time, only to discover we couldn't find them.

Of course, mother always disavowed playing any role in misplacing things. When I'd ask her where she might have put her glasses, she'd look at me wide-eyed and innocently, in shock and disbelief, as much as saying, Are you crazy; how should I know? Most of the time, they were staring us in the face, resting on a chair, on a table or on the vanity in the bathroom. But of course, in the evil way inanimate objects seem capable of conspiring against humans, we'd never see them right away. When we did, no thrill ever equaled finding something as mundane as a pair of glasses, just in the nick of time and just shy of despairing of ever doing so. All the frustration and recrimination vanish. You breathe a collective sigh of relief and hope it will never happen again. You even delude yourself into thinking you can do something to prevent a recurrence. But of course, the glasses, along with any

While it's typical for people with dementia, Alzheimer's, and similar conditions to misplace things, not all "misplacements" are the same, I concluded. Some things are simply accidentally hidden from view. Others, the more challenging, are intentionally hidden, sequestered as a result of paranoia. I discovered I had to adopt different strategies if there was going to be any hope of ever bringing "lost" objects to light.

number of other things, would vanish temporarily, again and again. And we would resume the hunt as inevitably.

Mother tended simply to misplace her glasses, casually leaving them lying around. But she consciously hid things like the TV remote or her favorite ring under her pillow or in a shoe, wrapped in toilet paper and often squirreled away under a piece of clothing in a drawer. I found a whole place setting underneath the sink in her bathroom. The pseudo-psychologist in me attributes these intentional hidings to my mother's almost constitutional craftiness, even slight paranoia, heightened by her deteriorating mental condition. But diagnoses don't matter when there's no cure for a condition, you feel helpless, and you're forever on the trail of missing necessities.

It takes someone thinking like someone paranoid to find something hidden by someone paranoid.

My strategy to find lost objects was to try to think like someone with dementia — more specifically, like my mother with dementia. Gradually, I realized there was a pattern to where she hid things, preferred places where I was almost assured I'd find *something*, even if it wasn't what I was looking for at a given moment. I used to ask myself, "If I were mother, where would I put the TV remote to hide it from me?" And more often than not, I'd find it — except not always. In the end, she hid the remote so well one time to this day I've never found it. On a more serious note, after I discovered she had been intentionally hiding my mail, including one envelope that contained a check for $750, I made sure she never got to the mailbox before I did.

Bizarre things I never thought could happen became the norm at home, and, even more bizarre, I even got used to them. I lost count of the number of times mother put her dress on backwards and how often I tried to persuade her to turn it around. I gave up begging her to change because she so adamantly refused and it simply wasn't worth the fight. After all, I realized that it didn't matter; the only thing that was important was at least she was wearing something clean. It wasn't harming her in any way. Besides, on backwards, a normal neckline morphed into a kind of mock mandarin collar — if not a major fashion statement at least a presentable one.

I even got used to finding food and assorted cutlery in the clothes dryer, though I wish I had become reconciled to that absurdity earlier than I did. Once at dinnertime, mother decided she couldn't finish her meal and made a beeline for the laundry room, opened the door to the clothes dryer, and was about to put her heaping dishful of food inside. I tried to stop her. Furious, she threw the dish on the floor.

You can do more harm by being confrontational and trying to stop an absurd action than by letting it run its course, as long as it won't hurt someone.

Because I handled the situation inappropriately, not only did I have an angry old lady who couldn't help herself to contend with, I had a mess (fortunately outside the dryer) to clean up. As I was picking up the pieces of dish and food, I realized there would have been no harm in my letting her put everything in the machine, then taking it out when she wasn't looking. In my defense, the first time it happened, I was still thinking of my mother as the rational and predictable person she had always been. Incredulous at what she was doing, it took me a while to adjust to our new reality. I would have plenty of time to learn, however, because the clothes dryer became a treasure trove of miscellaneous items.

After the fact, it's easy to laugh at all of the places where I found things out-of-place and to shrug off my memories of the topsy-turvy world in which I lived. But if I hadn't kept, and developed, my sense of humor *while* my mother was alive and up to her antics, I would have gone

I repeat myself because the message is so important: Laughter really is the best medicine for what ails the caregiver.

madder than the Mad Hatter. There was an impish quality to all of her unconscious and intentional hidings, and they provide some of my fondest memories of her — after all, I have the world's most special, and versatile, clothes dryer. More than once, when I've looked at it, I've chuckled, remembering the first time I found one of her sandwiches, carefully wrapped in a napkin, tucked away in there, as lovingly as, in more conscious days, she might have wrapped one of mine I couldn't finish and put in the refrigerator for me to eat later. The laughter such scenes provoke turns into a warm smile in my memory, a celebration of my mother as she had once been.

Anytime I wish, I can recall my wonderland of strange memories and stranger juxtapositions, which, like Alice, I would never want to forget, even though I still shake my head in disbelief.

16

REJECTING REJECTION

You've got to
Accent-tchu-ate the positive,
E-lim-my-nate the negative,
Latch on to the affirmative,
Don't mess with Mister In-between.
– Johnny Mercer

No, no, no — it's the worst word anyone trying to help someone else can hear, over and over again. Parents bemoan struggling through "the terrible twos" as their kids stake out their independence and fiendishly delight in rejecting everything. Not to minimize their frustration, but they know there's light at the end of *their* tunnel, when some yeses are sure eventually to creep into their conversation as their toddler experiments with affirmatives. They can also take comfort in thinking they have a bright, positive future to look forward to. Not so for this caregiver of a disapproving mother with dementia. I got used to being on the wrong side of a torrent of no's, with no realistic hope of the terrible tune ever changing for the better.

At one level, it was nothing new for me. My mother was a lifelong, hard-nosed skeptic. Initially, she greeted anything new, different, or strange by disapprovingly knitting her brow, chuckling, and dismissing it out-of-hand. The difference was, when she was rational and clear-headed, I could eventually reason with her or simply do what I wanted to with or without her blessing. Until I understood the game had forever changed, and I no longer enjoyed my usual options, I was unhappy and frustrated.

The more I listened, the more I discovered all of mother's no's were not created equal. Some were hard-and-fast and demanded my infinite patience and ultimate acceptance. Others were really yeses she couldn't voice, but it was my job to help her express. Before I learned how to distinguish the nuances between no's, I persisted when I should have changed my strategy or I gave up when I should have persisted — either way, I got into trouble I eventually figured out how to avoid.

Mother's hard-and-fast no-no's — the easiest to spot — were negatives from her ground-of-being no amount of coaxing or reasoning by anyone would

For both our sakes, I realized I needed to find a way to reject my mother's rejection and attempt to turn it positive without relying upon anything even remotely resembling reason. After careful study, I learned to listen for subtle nuances, cues and clues to distinguish among her routine negatives. Once I recognized them, I felt as though I discovered a whole new language — and in some ways I did. Anyone can do it.

ever turn positive. Typically, they were her visceral reaction to people whose very existences offended her (like the brother she detested) and subjects she regarded as too personal to be mentioned (like anything to do with bodily habits or sex), let alone discussed with, or in any way handled by, anyone else. Once, when I guaranteed I could maintain her privacy and still help her get into the shower and stand near her so she wouldn't fall, she turned livid at the mere thought — eyes wide open and threatening, fists shaking, jaw clenched — and let out a barrage of her most definitive no's. When I told her it was time to change her clothes, she would become irate. Even in her frailest frailty, she could fume, sputter — and hit.

Once, even when she appeared to be the frailest of frail, when I dared to lift the shoulder of her dress and tell her I could help her change into something clean, she bit me so hard on my left hand, she broke the skin — refusing to stop until I pleaded and pleaded with her. All I could think of was, if I tried to resist her in any way, her loose dental caps might fall out, and then we'd really be in a fix. Without a doubt, her bite was a no she really meant, worse than any bark.

Out of self-preservation, I discovered four ways to deal with no-no's.

First, I stopped trying to impose my will and let mother do things in her own time and in her own way — even if it meant putting up with something I couldn't stand or didn't think was appropriate. The fact she wasn't showering didn't matter, even though I may have thought she would feel so much better if she did. She was always clean, because she gave herself sponge-baths.

Second, I became a fatalist. I learned to trust things would eventually take care of themselves. And providence interceded in uncanny ways. Once, having given up hope of ever getting her to change a stained dress, which she would never have worn for a nanosecond had she been in her right mind, I was saved by a miracle: She spilled a glass of orange juice on herself and promptly made a beeline for her bedroom — to change! The devil in me thought I could have guaranteed she'd always be immaculately dressed, if I were willing to spill drinks on her from time to time when she needed to change. But my better nature would never have allowed me to carry out such a ruse.

Third, I became a master of stealth strategies — but only after enduring major heartache. Once, we were going out for (what should have been) a pleasant dinner. Mother dressed and looked great, except there was an obvious coffee stain on her white sweater. She went ballistic when I told her she couldn't wear it and should change it immediately. Even when I asked her to look in the mirror, she couldn't see the obvious, rather large, spot.

Eventually, she did change, but not before threatening to stay home. The incident ruined the evening. But I couldn't have avoided the blowup then, for no amount of reasoning or cajoling would have convinced her to change. And yet, I couldn't have simply looked the other way and let her go out looking as she did. In better days, she herself would never have appeared in public that way or allowed anyone else to do so. After that unfortunate incident, I figured out how to avoid any repeats. When she wasn't in her room, I removed the sweater and took it to the cleaners. She never knew the difference. From then on, on the sly, I routinely checked all her clothes to be sure they were wearable — and had them cleaned as necessary.

Fourth, there were times when, regrettably, I had to impose my will in extreme circumstances. Fortunately, they were few and far between. Once mother walked out of the house into the street and refused to come inside. To no avail, I tried to reason with her. I couldn't allow her to put herself at risk, no matter what I had to do. Physically parrying her moves, I got her back into the driveway. But she still refused to come inside. I was on the verge of picking her up and bringing her in, when she relented. After that incident and another one when she might have gone out at night, I had a second set of locks installed high enough on all outside doors so she couldn't let herself out. She was never in any danger of being locked in if there were an emergency, because they could only be bolted from the inside, and she was never alone from then on.

On balance, more of my mother's no's were yeses just waiting for me to help her express.

When I realized many of my mother's no's were really yeses she couldn't get unstuck from no-mode, I learned simply to ignore them, persist a bit, and she'd always come around. They were her first, automatic responses to my offers of anything, but I eventually knew not to take them seriously. In the theatre of the absurd in which I found myself living, there was even a positive side to her losing her memory — and I relied upon it to get from no to yes more than once. Sometimes she took one look at the food I had prepared for her, announced, in disgust, she couldn't eat it, and scurried back to her room. But I knew there was always a yes on the other side of *that* no. Relying upon her guaranteed forgetfulness, I'd give her a few minutes to settle down and then announce

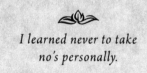

I learned never to take no's personally.

with a great flourish dinner was ready. She'd promptly get up, walk arm-in-arm with me — and eat to her heart's content the very meal she had rejected minutes before.

I started out by rejecting my mother's rejection of my positive efforts to help her. I ended up rejecting my hurt feelings when she rejected me. Until I did so, I took her jibes personally — and overreacted. As awful as it was to hear no after no after no, eventually, I embraced my mother's negativity as a welcome sign of the life still left in her. In that context, getting from no to yes was less important than it first appeared to be.

In the end, as a caregiver, I learned to take whatever I got, work with it as best I could, and hope to be able to turn as many negatives as I could into positives — or get over them.

17

CAREGIVING FOR MOTHER'S SOUL

Give the lady what she wants!
– Marshall Field

Caregiving for my mother's physical needs was relatively easy. She had minimal aches and pains. She wasn't confined to a wheelchair and didn't have to use a walker. Until the last three or four weeks of her life, she walked faster than most people half her age. She showed no signs of osteoporosis, took only one low-dose pill for high blood pressure, and attended to all her personal needs. My job was to be vigilant: to be sure she didn't fall or otherwise harm herself, to look for signs she might need medical attention she wouldn't or couldn't ask for herself. I could almost always take care of her physical needs with a home remedy, over-the-counter ointment, a protein drink, or bit of exercise.

The person you see is not the person your family member may really be. I learned to see and treat my mother like the woman she had always been, not like the person she had outwardly become. When I treated her as though her current limitations did not exist, she blossomed, as though on cue.

Caregiving for mother's soul required a unique kind and level of nourishment. I'm not referring to doing anything to nurture her spiritual life or guarantee her place in heaven by cleansing her earthly being of sin, but nourishing her inner being while she was still alive so she still felt like a human being, not an object. The part of her I tried to reach is who we all are when we're talking to ourselves, running the script of our hopes, expectations, and desires — the innermost part of our being that truly makes us uniquely who we are.

Three magical phrases I discovered invariably brought a smile to my mother's face and a nod of blissful recognition. Taken together they prove love, a cup of kindness, is the best medicine — and, no matter how "out of it" mother appeared to be, there were ways to reach her.

No matter how detached mother seemed from reality, guaranteed, I could always connect with her by appealing to her vanity. After the first time I saw how radiantly she lit up when I told her how beautiful she looked, I

The first magical, soul-tapping phrase was my saying, "You look so beautiful today."

peppered her day with compliments. Every morning when I went into her room, I would kiss her. Her hair would be disheveled, of course. But I would tell her how pretty her eyes were and how soft her skin was. I would say how the color of what she was wearing brought out the green or blue in her eyes and how nice her hair looked after she brushed it. My comment about hair was an out-and-out lie, but her eyes *really* never lost their glimmer and her skin was remarkably taut, if not wrinkle-free, for a woman nearly 90.

She positively glowed at my flattery — shaking her head slightly, fluttering her eyelashes, and raising both her hands as though brushing my compliments off in a gesture of humility. Just under five feet, mother always said she wished she were taller. Knowing if I said anything about her height I could get a rise out of her, I would even tell her she looked as though she were growing and add she walked remarkably straight. She *did* walk straight. Openly amused at my suggestion she was getting taller, she'd revel enough in the joke to have the last laugh. She'd giggle and

The second magical phrase I used to reach her soul was, "You are always such a good person."

thrust her shoulders back in an effort to make herself look even taller.

No matter how mentally fuzzy she might have seemed, she'd always come alive when I told her what a good person she was. Then, obviously aching for my compliment, she'd ask, "Why?" My answer would thrill her: "Because you always loved other people and tried to be kind and do the right thing." "Yes," she would answer, touched to the depths of her inner being.

I was telling her the truth — and I absolutely knew she knew it. And that's why, I think, those words got through to her so effectively. I didn't have to mention specific, endearing scenarios I knew from her lifetime of being "a good person." But I suspect this particular magical phrase awakened them in *her* well of memory. She had endless examples from which she could pick.

I'm guessing my words jogged her into remembering how, in her whole life, she was never impressed by what others owned, where they lived, the car they drove, or any of the externals that typically dazzle so many people they lose their moral compass. I'm guessing I was able to awaken the love she expressed that extended beyond family and friends to strangers, most of whom she never saw more than once. Like me, perhaps she remembered how, at holidays, she always made a place at the dinner table for anyone she discovered had no place to go.

Perhaps, she remembered Elizabeth Boyd, our housekeeper in Connecticut, whom she treated like a sister and whose death devastated her. They were the oddest couple — a 6'3" tall black woman who chewed tobacco and a Jewish woman less than 5 feet. Elizabeth figuratively looked up to my mother; my mother literally and figuratively never looked down on her. I also hope my words awakened her memory of a little hillbilly girl who lived in a shack with her family at the edge of the woods near the suburban homes like ours which would eventually displace them. To my embarrassment, mother always stopped to give that kid a ride to school. To her, the child was as sacred as every human being, no less than any of us who didn't want to be seen with her. And for such a profound act of compassion alone, she deserved to hear "You were *always* such a good person."

Telling my mother people loved her was caregiving for her soul. After starting with "I love you," I'd fill in the blank, clarifying the everybody with a string of once-familiar names: Harry (my father) loves you, Stephen (me, by

The third magical phrase that did the trick was, "Everybody loves you."

name, because when I said I alone I couldn't be certain she would make the connection) loves you, Fred (my brother) loves you, Helen (our housekeeper) loves you, Ida (her deceased mother) loves you. Over and over I'd repeat the mantra. How she lit up when I told her everyone loved her, even when she was practically in a coma. "Yes," she would reply with all the breath she had left — until finally all she could do was sigh.

In addition to the magical phrases, I tried anything and everything to stimulate mother's senses, hoping doing so might reactivate her brain cells. I foolishly showed her old photographs to try to jog her memory. Most didn't, but I stopped when I realized the few she recognized only awakened sad thoughts of people whom she

Dancing and music reached my mother, no matter how distant she might have appeared to be. It was the key to her soul. I wish I had done more of it.

knew had died. She delighted in my playing some of her favorite songs on the piano, though she could no longer sing along as she used to. She always loved to dance. She taught me the box-step and the cha-cha and made sure I learned ballroom dancing as a kid. Sometimes, as I escorted her to the kitchen for a meal, I would carefully guide her — she was so, so frail — in a ballroom step or two, and she would beam.

You can always reach another soul by speaking from yours.

Music, dancing, and those magical phrases got through to my mother's inner self like nothing else. A doctor may prescribe a pill which needs to be taken once a day or every four hours or whatever — no more, no less. But anyone can administer infusions of love to the soul 24/7, with absolutely no fear of overdosing. Don't hesitate, always give more than you think is enough, and don't stop. The prescription allows endless refills.

18

DYING BY DESIGN

I am the master of my fate:
I am the captain of my soul.
– W. E. Henley

In December 2003, my mother underwent an emergency appendectomy. In typical fashion, she said nothing about the excruciating pain in her side until it was unbearable and on the verge of rupturing. But when she finally got out of bed and dragged herself into the kitchen, bent over, and owned up to it, I took her to the emergency room.

If it's any kind of real emergency, never take anyone to an emergency room yourself. Always call 911. My mother was seen pretty quickly when I drove her to the hospital, but I realize now I should have called for an ambulance as I did on future occasions. She would have been admitted and seen immediately, instead of having to wait in the waiting room.

For the four-and-a-half years after her appendectomy, my mother slowly went downhill. She was physically strong, but gradually became weaker, and her memory began to fade. Four days in May 2008 changed our lives, however. At about 6:30 one morning, my mother seemed fine when I looked in on her. But about an hour later, when I returned, I saw she had soiled herself. I woke her so I could help her to the bathroom, where I hoped she could clean herself while I changed the sheets. The night before she was perfectly capable of getting up on her own and tending to her needs, though she had been listless during the day, preferred to stay in bed, and seemed to have pain on her right side. But that fateful morning, she was barely able to stand — and couldn't walk. It seemed obvious to me she had suffered a mild stroke.

That time, I knew to call 911. I shall *always* remember the relief I felt when I heard the operator say, "Help is on the way." Doctors confirmed that my mother had had a slight stroke. At the end of a few days in the hospital, she was still unable to walk. To get her the best care under the circumstances, she went to a skilled rehab center for a few weeks before coming home. There, she would receive daily physical therapy and be watched round-the-clock. I even thought she might benefit from being around so many different people for a change, instead of staying at home, mostly with me.

Mission accomplished! She appeared perfectly happy in the rehab facility. And when she returned home, she was able to walk on her own. The day I picked her up, as soon as she walked into the kitchen, she ate heartily and proceeded confidently back to her room — knowing exactly where she was going — preferring to take my arm instead of the walker I tried to get her accustomed to using to prevent her from falling. But from then on, there were good days and bad days. She had physical therapy at home, but it would tire her out. She was terribly weak and would barely eat. She had become incontinent.

But even in her debilitated state, my strong-willed mother proved, ultimately, she was the master of her fate. About two weeks before she died, she wrested control of her caregiving from me, for good. Frail and weak, but still with an all-knowing, resolute twinkle in her eye, she sat at the edge of her bed, looked me squarely in the eyes, totally at peace with herself and, out of the relentless mist of her dementia, said, clearly and strongly, "I'm tired, and I can't do anything more for my children."

At that moment, I knew my mother had decided to die and was saying goodbye in the only way she knew how. My brother and I were all she lived for. Once she had come to the conclusion she couldn't do anything more for her children, the tireless, devoted mother felt she had no reason to live.

I remembered reading in hospice literature how important it is to give someone permission to die and how odd and impossible such heartless advice had sounded at the time. Until it was *my* mother actually telling me *she* was ready to die and I was the one saying the unthinkable — that it was okay with me — I never believed I would face such a situation or could say such a thing. And yet, somehow I did. In fact, I felt if I didn't tell her it was okay with me, I would be failing her at the most crucial moment of her life, our lives.

Desperately fighting to hold back the flood of my tears about to erupt, with an almost clinical matter-of-factness, I looked her in the eyes and said, "I know, I know. You did everything for your children. I love you. Stephen loves you. [As usual, I said both I and Stephen because she didn't know me by name, so I had to be sure she heard my name, especially at such a delicate time.] And Fred [my brother] loves you. You were the best mother anyone could have had."

Then, I kissed her and put my arms around the wisp of a body that was left of her once vital frame and, with tears streaming down my face, but trying to keep her from seeing them, I told her I knew she was tired—and it was okay for her to go. I told her I would always love her, I would miss her more than I could ever say, and I would never forget her.

After the most surreal experience of my life, she put her little head on the pillow and took a nap. For the first time in the longest time, she wasn't agitated or confused. She seemed totally calm and content — and I did, too. Both devastated and relieved at coming to terms with the inevitable, I left her to her sleep. I can't remember what I did for the next few hours. But nothing really mattered after those brief, at once devastating and curiously freeing, moments. Our lives had changed irrevocably. For the next 10 days, I watched her slow, steady, and predictable decline, knowing what only the two of us knew: her end was near, and it was entirely her choice.

According to her wishes, she was eventually under the care of hospice. There were no tubes, forced feeding, or heroics — only palliative care. Eventually bed-ridden, she remained at home. And, in addition to hospice, I arranged for private-duty, round-the-clock care.

The slow decline of her last days was peaceful. The only pain was mine in seeing her fade

I followed my mother's orders about how she wanted end-of-life decisions made for her. She signed a living will, appointed me her healthcare surrogate, and specifically said she wanted to be allowed to die naturally. I knew from our discussions about death and dying, as well as from how she dealt with my father's last months, what I should and should not do. Caregiving, I knew, was not about my imposing my will upon her, but about respecting her wishes to the end — especially at the end.

and knowing the minutes were ticking away and it was just a question of when, not if, she would die. But the eeriest thing of all was realizing my "rational" planning eleven years before was unfolding precisely as I wanted it to: Mother had lived with me for the last decade of her life, safe and protected, we had the financial resources to provide the best possible care, we had avoided any serious crises, her dignity was maintained, and she was surrounded by people who loved her.

I watched mother nature take my mother. Or, more accurately, my mother give in to mother nature. Or, since any struggle to stay alive was over, I had to think they really were operating in tandem, one and the same at that point. From then on, her death unfolded with textbook predictability.

First, she stopped eating. I had gone out for an important business meeting, but went into her room to tell her I'd soon be back. She was delighted with the way I was dressed — for my entire life reserving the right to criticize, especially my choice of colors — but approving wholeheartedly this time. Helen Vinson stayed with her, especially trying to get her to eat her lunch. But when I returned, she told me mother didn't touch a morsel. I tried to feed her, without success — a very bad sign, because I was always able to get her to eat something, even if no one else was.

From then on, she ate no solid food. I knew the end was near when she stopped drinking on her own a few days later. Unable to hold a glass, she had been using a straw, but then she didn't even have the strength to sip. Eventually, she could only take liquid from the syringe one of us would place in her mouth. At first, we tried ice chips but the cold shocked her and they were messy, because she had a hard time keeping them in her mouth, so they melted and dripped out.

On day nine, she was barely conscious. I asked the nurse if she had put up her usual fight when she tried to bathe her, but she said no. At that point, I knew she was still breathing but practically gone. Her final act maintaining the dignity she so prized was only willingly to consent to the unthinkable invasion of her privacy when it could no longer violate her ground of being.

Friday, June 27, 2008, I went into mother's room at about 7:30 a.m. The young woman on the night shift was standing by her bed. When I asked her how long my mother had been making a strange, guttural noise from her throat, she told me it had just started. Though I had never heard the sound before, instantly, I knew it was "the death rattle," the chilling signal of her final breaths. After I called hospice and described

In my estimation, I waited too long to call hospice to discuss options — until just about two-and-a-half weeks before my mother died. Until then, she was functioning pretty well on her own, and I had no reason to think she would go downhill so quickly. At that point, I was looking only for general information, instinctively knowing to prepare. I waited as long as I did asking them actually to intervene, even when she was obviously fading, because doing so felt too much like admitting she was dying. I just couldn't bring myself to do it, until it really looked like the end was near, and frankly I was exhausted, about 10 days before she died.

I am apparently typical of most people. Carol Bradley Bursack, editor-in-chief of ElderCarelink, reports that a billboard in her city reads, "Most families say, 'Why did we wait so long to call hospice?'" So what's not too long? Typically, people may qualify for hospice if they are certified to be terminal within six months.

Whenever they are called, in my experience, hospice is wonderful. They supplied an electrified hospital bed which could be raised and lowered for my mother's comfort and our easy reach of her. It had an automatically inflating and deflating pad under the sheet to keep her from developing bed sores. And of course, hospice nurses came to take her vital signs and aides came to bathe her. Most important, they were there with their unique kind of support for my mother and me, giving both of us the compassionate care we needed at the most trying time in our lives.

my mother's condition, they immediately sent a nurse, who beckoned me into the hall and confirmed "it" would be soon.

I went back into my mother's room and reached for her hand, to reassure her I was there, expecting as usual to feel her vice-like fist tightening around my fingers. Until the day before she died, even when she appeared to be semi-comatose, she firmly gripped my hand, holding on, as though for dear life, without wanting to let go — as if to assure me she knew I was there and to reassure me she was still alive. But for the first time, her hand was cold and lifeless. Lost forever was the warmth of my mother's touch that had always made everything better throughout my life. I had felt death.

As real and undeniable as the empty feeling in her hand was, I couldn't grasp the idea that she was more dead than alive. But less than an hour later, just before noon, she died — finally letting go completely, by her own design, with the same uncanny determination that got her through everything in her life and made her the consummate — and tireless — daughter, wife, mother, and friend.

At the foot of her bed, my mother always kept the woolen blanket she knitted to cover my baby carriage. Until shortly before she died, she covered herself with it when she napped, as though enshrouding herself in the warmth of her past, when she was joyfully expecting her first-born. Long before anyone knew how to test for the sex of an embryo, expectant mothers hedged their bets. It was gray and pink.

Even in her foggiest moments, I have no doubt she absolutely knew the blanket was her handiwork — and remained proud of knitting it. When I would say, "You made this," she would agree and point to where the alternating, cable-stitched panels had been joined to the others. Her never having lost touch with that faded fabric was the most poignant and indisputable proof my mother's *real* self was always "there" in spite of what her dementia might have camouflaged.

I couldn't imagine to whom I could give that emotion-filled carriage cover after mother died. To anyone who didn't know its history, or care to find out, it would have looked like a rag — to be disposed of, not cherished. Because I couldn't allow it to be desecrated, I had it cremated with her body. It seemed only fitting that what was still there for her when she appeared not still to be there for us would be with her forever.

19

PLANNING FOR "CONTINUITY OF CARE"— OR NOT!

Be Prepared.
– Motto of the Boy Scouts of America

My whole life has been about successful planning. I've always had a vivid picture in my mind of what I've wanted to accomplish — and have pretty much gotten it or known the reason why not. After being a caregiver, I discovered the limits of my foresight and how close I might have come to tripping myself up — and I didn't like it one bit. To other caregivers, forewarned is forearmed.

Somewhat cavalierly, I planned the steps leading up to my mother's moving in with me, and it didn't surprise me when they unfolded according to script. As a trends analyst for many years, I studied the characteristics and needs of America's aging population. One fact stood out more than any other: after 80, people experience a natural decline. I never told my mother what I had learned. But right after her 79th birthday, I began diplomatically paving the way for her to accept the idea of selling her condo and living with me.

Once we were together, my planning became more serious and long-term. The one thought constantly running through my mind was making sure my mother would have whatever care she needed for the rest of her life. First and foremost, I would never have put her in a nursing home, even though she told me more than once, if she needed continual care, she would *want* it, not just prefer it. For me, her wish was simply out-of-the-question. I had to overrule it, though I never told her I did. I was actually being more selfish than noble. Knowing myself, if she weren't living with me, I would always have been anxious about her — wondering if and how strangers were caring for her, how she was feeling, what I could or should be doing for her. It was easier on me to have her where I could watch her and the care she was receiving.

Having made my decision to keep my mother at home, I planned to convert the room next to hers into a bedroom for live-in, paid staff, if her condition warranted it. I would have torn down the wall separating both rooms or cut out a doorway or, at the very least, installed an intercom. The major hurdle I imagined under that scenario would have been getting her to allow a stranger to invade her privacy — bathing, dressing, and feeding her. But I also figured, if she needed such a basic level of care, she'd be willing to accept the help — or at least I hoped so.

My first wake-up call testing my ability to ensure the continuity of mother's care began as a terrifying scare, which caught me completely off-guard. It was a day like any other day. I had gone into her room to tell her dinner was ready. But, sitting at the edge of her bed, she told me she couldn't stand up. Thinking it was just because her bed was low, I gave her my arm to help her up. But once she stood up with some difficulty, she simply couldn't walk. Terrified that she had had a stroke, I had learned immediately to call 911. According to the doctor in the emergency room, she was just dehydrated, which I couldn't believe and which made me feel as though I had somehow neglected her. They gave her liquid intravenously. She came home at 10:30 p.m. and even ate the food I had prepared for her four hours earlier.

Happily, our first scare turned out to be a manageable alarm and not a major crisis. It alerted me to how the simplest thing I would never even have imagined could seriously affect a fragile, older person. I made sure from then on she drank enough liquids. As important, it made me seriously begin to think about planning for a worst-case scenario. What if it *had been* a stroke, I asked myself? The only answer I could come up with was that she would come home and I would have someone take care of her round-the-clock. Planning ahead, I started asking people who might know of potential, live-in caregivers for advice. And, in my mind, I began tearing down the north wall of my mother's room.

My second wake-up call also began as a terrifying scare. Early one morning, I went into her room to check on her, only to discover that she couldn't walk and appeared disoriented. This time, I was *certain* she had had a minor stroke. I again called 911. She was admitted to the hospital, and doctors confirmed my suspicion. At the end of a few days' stay, I had a choice to make. But this time, circumstances narrowed my choices and took away my feeling of being in control. It was a first for me and didn't sit at all well.

Still unable to walk steadily, my mother could have come home and have had a physical therapist visit her, or she could have gone into a rehab center, where she would receive daily therapy and 24-hour care. As devastating as the thought of her going into rehab was for me, I accepted it because it provided the most and best care, it was only going to be for about three weeks, and the center was close to my house.

I used the time my mother was in rehab to plan for the next stage in her care. I knew, from then on, she would need assistance with daily living. My housekeeper, who had worked in a nursing home, agreed to increase her schedule to five days a week to care mostly for my mother. I arranged for a caring and especially well-qualified aide in the rehab center to cover the rest of the week on her days off. But I knew my mother was fading. So, my brother and I met with our family doctor and he put her under hospice, which had *always* been part of the plan, completely in keeping with my mother's wishes. In addition, we arranged for round-the-clock, private duty, in-home care, which she received until she died.

The wisdom in the paraphrase of Robert Burns's words, "The best-laid plans of mice and men go oft awry," keeps going through my mind. As much planning as I did, I failed to plan in the most important way, however. It never occurred to me I wouldn't be alive to oversee my mother's care. I never sat down with my brother to discuss who would have cared for her — and how — if I had died before she did. My mother had her own resources. She was also the primary beneficiary of my estate. No matter how long she lived, she could always have received the best care money could buy.

But only now, I realize we had no plan for what her care without me would actually have been. My caregiving plan focused on a beginning: Moving my mother in with me. My mother's own plan focused on the end: She had a living will and designated me her healthcare surrogate. She had made legal and financial provisions for her estate years before she died. She wanted to be cremated.

But none of us thought about writing a plan for the all-important "middle" time, the extent and condition of which none of us could predict. By sheer luck, we proved Robert Burns wrong and our "best laid plans" did not go "awry." But they could easily and unhappily have done so — and yet have been so easily avoided.

For their and their family members' good, wise caregivers should always be out to prove the Boy Scouts right—and Robert Burns wrong.

Every family should develop its formal caregiving plan —
to avoid crises limiting your ability to make decisions when you
really need maximum flexibility to make the right choices. Not
thinking ahead ties your hands and makes you a potentially
tragic victim of circumstances.
It goes without saying every adult in your family should sign wills,

living wills, healthcare surrogates, durable powers of attorney, and
any other documents directly or indirectly affecting the caregiving
they may need. In addition, everyone who may be involved in
caregiving should have copies or know where the originals are kept.

Your family plan should be a carefully thought-out strategy — in
writing — and kept current, obviously well ahead of your ever
needing it. It should include a list of things to do to handle any
emergency, with phone numbers of everyone who needs to be
contacted. Early decisions during an emergency may have a direct
bearing on someone's eventual caregiving needs.

For example, if someone does not wish to be resuscitated after
suffering a massive stroke, but is because written instructions were
not given to emergency medical personnel, a family may be put
through the agony of having to request he be taken off the life-
support to which he should never have been attached. Or, if she
was resuscitated but not put on life support, her family may face
years of caregiving costs keeping someone alive who is in a coma
or seriously handicapped and who expressly said she never wanted
to be in such a state.

Your plan should include options to facilitate caregiving at home,
well before the need may arise — like determining the space you
have or which would have to be built to accommodate someone,
the cost and extent to which you can retrofit your existing living
space by widening doors to accommodate wheelchairs and
assistive devices, as well as installing simple things like safety bars
in showers and tubs. If you're someone who really thinks ahead and
were to build a new home, you would be in the enviable position of
being able to include those and other caregiving-friendly elements in
your new construction.

It is also crucial for everyone in a family to decide who will be
responsible for "care and feeding" when a family member needs
it. To facilitate decision-making when the time comes, one person
needs to be designated in charge well beforehand. But having a
single point-person shouldn't relieve anyone of some measure of

involvement, simply clarify lines of authority. Planning ahead will enable you to provide the best and most appropriate care and allow you to feel and be in charge when you are most likely to be overwhelmed and at the effect of events — and when the last thing you want is to feel powerless and the unhappy victim of circumstances.

20

GAINING MY FREEDOM
BY GIVING IT UP

I have found among its other benefits,
giving liberates the soul of the giver.
– Maya Angelou

To most adult sons and daughters, the mere *thought* of having an elderly parent move in with them, let alone having it actually happen, is somewhere between inconceivable and anathema. If they have a family, they simply cannot imagine the adjustments everyone would have to make. If they live alone, they can't imagine giving up their coveted independence. I can fully understand their hesitation and concern, as well as their ultimate decision not to take on the responsibility. Many families are dysfunctional, at best; some blood relatives don't even speak to one another. The thought of living under the same roof often seems out-of-the-question.

No surprise then, when I told friends and relatives my mother was going to move in with me, or had already done so, almost everyone asked me, "How could you give up your freedom and privacy?" I don't know what they thought I was doing with my life — walking around my house naked, traveling the globe at will, participating in orgies, or whatever else defined my "freedom and privacy" for them. For me, it was actually a bigger deal to convince my mother to give up *her* "freedom and privacy" than for me to do so. *She* was the one who had to rationalize moving in with her son when she was still strong and independent. *She* was the one who had to convince her friends and relatives she was still capable of living on her own and wasn't giving up for any reason.

The truth is, I was actually acting selfishly when I invited my mother to move in. I believed I was gaining a lion's share of emotional and psychological freedom, not losing anything. By giving up my personal space and any freedom that came with it, I saw myself gaining peace-of-mind, a different, but infinitely more important, freedom. Once my mother was living with me, I knew I would no longer have to worry about where she was, if she had fallen or otherwise harmed herself, if she was taking care of herself, if someone was trying to take advantage of her — all the things that used to prey on my mind.

Round-the-clock family caregiving can turn into the most productive experience anyone can have. It's a way of wiping the boards of all extraneous endeavors and people, the best excuse for getting out of the time-wasting, energy-draining, going-through-the-motions activities that consume so many people. In short, it can be a way of concentrating your energies and discovering what's really important, productive, and rewarding. And it all comes about as a result of meeting someone else's needs. It's proof of the irony: the more you give up, the more you gain.

Of course, the last thing in the world I ever imagined was that to care for my mother, I would, eventually, have to give up my physical free-dom and be confined to what might have appeared like house arrest or quasi-solitary confinement to an outsider looking in. If anyone had told me I would, for more than four years, spend every day at home — getting out for at most an hour to shop for food, but most days never leaving — I would never have believed them or thought I could handle it. Single, with no family responsibilities, I was used to leading my life completely on my terms, coming and going as I pleased. Plus, when mother moved in, I couldn't imagine her ever needing — or allowing herself to need — anything, anybody else, or me. My picture of her my whole life was as a strong woman who always took care of everyone else. And, in the early years of our living together, nothing appeared to have changed.

But in fact, gradually, during about the last four years of her life, mother slowly declined. Her dependence upon me, and my completely devoting my life to her, progressed so imperceptibly I didn't even know it was happening. It all unfolded naturally. Each phase required minor adjustments I easily made. I accepted her as my all encompassing, number one priority without even knowing I was doing so. When she stopped driving, I simply did the grocery shopping she had routinely done. After all, before she moved in, I did it. It was no sweat. Because she was no longer able to prepare her own food, let alone mine, I cooked for both of us. Again, no problem, for I always cooked for myself when I lived alone. Eventually, when she was no longer comfortable staying alone at home at night, I never went out unless my brother could visit for the evening, because she wouldn't let anyone else stay with her. When I was no longer comfortable with her staying at home alone even during the day, I almost never went out — and then only for an *absolutely* necessary reason — unless she had just started taking a nap and I knew she wouldn't be up for at least an hour. Eventually, I would never leave her for a minute unless someone else was at home.

But what I finally lost in physical freedom, I gained in both personal and professional liberty. My transition from freewheeling individual to homebound caregiver was easier for me than it might have been for others. For years, computers and the Internet allowed me to run my professional life entirely from my home office. As a writer and consultant, I routinely emailed manuscripts to publishers. I found phone conference calls infinitely more productive and practical than face-to-face meetings — and the only way to go anyway when clients' principals were in different cities. I was still able to do everything I needed and wanted to — and continue to earn a living. In fact, I became even more productive and profitable because my time was completely my own. By circumstances and choice, I couldn't and wouldn't waste any time going out for anything but the most pressing business matter. And if I absolutely had to meet face-to-face with people but couldn't get away, I'd invite them in for lunch or dinner.

In between writing and taking care of other business during the day, of course I talked with my mother, cooked for us, and attended to her needs. She spent her days eating, watching TV, and taking care of her personal needs — as well as reading and finishing crossword puzzles and word jumbles in ink, until her dementia prevented her from doing so. We spent quality time together each and every night. I set aside evenings exclusively for her (us)—usually from about 7 p.m. to until 10 or 11 p.m., whenever she began to doze off.

Routinely, after dinner, we would go into her room and watch TV. We talked and laughed and genuinely enjoyed each other's company. I was delighted to see, even with her mild dementia, she could follow plots and understand jokes. She always had an uncanny ability to know where a plot was leading and who the *real* villain was. We had developed a line-up of shows she particularly enjoyed, principally reruns, like the British comedy *Are You Being Served?*, *M.A.S.H.*, and *Walker, Texas Ranger*. She delighted in the British, social climbing Hyacinth Bucket (pronounced bouquet!), the cross-dressing antics of Corporal Max Klinger and the kickboxing exploits of Chuck Norris.

Ever a multi-tasker, I put our quality time to ultra-productive use by studying Spanish vocabulary and grammar, an obsession of mine for years. Because I was memorizing and reviewing kernels of information, not following a story line or a train of thought, I could also hold a conversation and follow what we were watching on TV at the same time.

My being homebound even gave me significant social freedom. I began having more and more luncheons and dinner parties at home. As a result, I became a better cook and host than I'd ever been. Sometimes, before she began noticeably to fade, my mother would genuinely participate in the festivities. I never felt isolated, because I am a loner by nature. Giving up going out at night was no hardship for me: I didn't have, or look for, compelling reasons to socialize in the first place and always found idle chatter draining. Instead, I turned *having* to stay at home into a truly positive experience. I saw only the people I wanted to see. Everyone understood why I couldn't accept invitations to go out and came to my dinner parties, without feeling they had to reciprocate. On balance, I think I had a more active, and enjoyable, social life than I had had in years.

Ironically, during the two or more years when my comings and goings were most limited, I was more productive and enjoyed my greatest freedom. I published more of my writing than I had at any other time. I had more clients. I gave more speeches and seminars than ever. By staying almost nonstop at home, I had no time for the small talk and wasteful office politics consuming so many people in business. Because it was such a hassle for me to arrange to go out of the house, let alone travel any distance, I only went where I absolutely had to and where it was most profitable, and I only accepted

The ultimate lesson of my caregiving is that real *freedom doesn't come from being able to do what you want; it comes from doing what you* choose *to do. Because caring for my mother was totally my choice, it was at once the most confining but, ultimately, the most liberating experience of my life. When I appeared to give up my freedom, I actually got more of it than I had ever had or could have imagined possible.*

invitations from people with whom I genuinely wanted to socialize.

To this day, even though my mother died and I am theoretically free to return to my freewheeling days, I have remained a recluse by choice. But when and if the spirit moves me, I could just as easily break out of my shell.

21

TAMING MY GUILTY IMAGINATION

It's only those who do nothing that
make no mistakes, I suppose.
– Joseph Conrad

Whenever people learned my mother was living with me and receiving all my attention, especially as she declined, they would tell me what a wonderful thing I was doing — and how few people would do the same for their family members. When she died, I received notes, telling me what a wonderful son I had been. Frankly, those cut me to the quick. I broke down every time I read them.

Of course, I appreciated the thought behind their praise, but I didn't feel I deserved it. I know everyone meant well. But honestly, I didn't feel wonderful. I never felt I was doing anything special. For me, it couldn't have been any other way. The kind words I received from others simply reinforced the anguish I felt for not having done more. When my mother was alive, I felt guilty for not having found a way to keep her strong and reverse her downward slide. And when she died, I felt I flat-out failed her. Yes, she had lived until 90. But I would have wanted her to live longer — and better, of course. How long? I had no idea. How much better? I didn't know that either.

Much of my guilt was because I felt I had to wing it. Deep down I wasn't absolutely certain I had done the right things. It's not as if there were some universally accepted, guaranteed foolproof method or recipe for caregiving I simply had to follow. I asked professionals questions about nutrition, exercise, Alzheimer's, dementia, and other topics and issues. But no one ever said to me, "Do this, and this, and that—and you will have done everything you possibly could to be the best caregiver." If anything, however well-intentioned they may have been, the fuzziness of too many professionals about even the most basic matters suggested they also were groping for answers. One nurse told me my mother's condition was "only going to get worse." But she couldn't say when or exactly how. So, replaying my caregiving years, I felt guilty for not having found someone who could have been more specific about her inevitable decline.

Part of my guilt also stemmed from eventually having to face my limits as a caregiver and protector. After 10 years, the hardest thing for me to accept was, in the end, I alone would not be able to give my mother the level of care she needed. Even though we had the financial resources to provide her round-the-clock care when she needed it in the last weeks of her life, I hated having to let strangers see her in so debilitated a condition. Until then, the full extent of her deterioration was known only to my brother and me — and a few trusted friends and relatives. I wanted to save her from the prying, judgmental eyes of strangers who would dismiss her as just another demented, old lady, no matter how compassionate they might have tried to appear to be.

In odd moments, after my mother died, random regrets continued to dart in and out of my mind. I wished I had found the key to getting her out of the house more often. I used to take her to her favorite Thai restaurant almost every Sunday, but eventually she refused to go — why, she never said. I wished I'd pressed her and found out why so we could perhaps have continued going there. When she stopped driving, I took her shopping for clothes. Then, she said she didn't want to bother going any longer, because she never found anything she liked and lamented that all the styles changed and there was nothing "for her." I never found a way even to get her to agree to take advantage of a sale, which in better days would surely have motivated her. I wished I had insisted on taking her to visit her few remaining friends, or I'd arranged for them to visit her. I stopped suggesting such visits because she always nixed them. She genuinely appeared not to care about seeing anyone. But I couldn't help thinking I could have found a way to get her some measure of social contact and keep her from being so isolated.

I wish I had found more recipes and explored more ways to prepare food she could eat. Perhaps, she would have eaten more and remained stronger longer, I thought, if I had cooked better — especially during the last few years of her life, when she could only eat soft food. Now, when it's too late, I can think of a thousand palatable, easy-to-swallow dishes I could have prepared. Sometimes, I think I should have eaten with her more often, except, when I did and said how delicious the food was, she would sigh, roll her eyes, and tell me it was terrible. Recoiling from her negativity, I concluded it was usually better to leave her alone. But I had a gnawing feeling I made the wrong choice.

I wish I'd gotten her to exercise. I should have made it a regular routine to walk outside with her and found ways to overcome her immediate, categorical refusal to do so. I wish I had slept in her room when she went to the hospital for the last time. I got angry with myself for ever having gotten angry at my mother, though I have the comfort of knowing I never showed my displeasure to her. Sometimes she did things so negative, so unappreciative, and so spiteful, I would simply excuse myself and grouse to myself far away from her. I know it's human to get plugged in from time to time. But I didn't like losing my cool — even in private.

If I hadn't figured out how to cope with my wild, self-accusing imagination, I would be living a life of perpetual regret—like other well meaning but too often frustrated caregivers. It took me a while, but

I finally found the thought that liberated me from self-incrimination:
that at the time I made every decision on my mother's behalf, I believed
I was doing the right thing, the best thing, the only appropriate thing.
No matter how much time, energy, or money was involved, I intended
to provide her with the best possible care—and I did. Hell may be
filled with good intentions, but so I believe may the other place. I knew
my motives were unassailable. Only with that self-assurance was I
finally able to tame my guilty imagination, to celebrate having taken
on a responsibility I never knew I had the guts to fulfill—and to move
on with my life. Such a level of commitment is surely the most anyone
should have expected from me or I could have expected from myself.

Yes, from time to time, I still mull over my regrets, but I am armed with strong defenses to tame my guilty imagination — and give myself a break.

22

REVERSING ROLE-REVERSAL

Do you know anyone who would — secretly, sincerely, in his innermost self — really prefer to return to childhood?
– Anita Desai

I wish I had a proverbial dollar for every time someone spouted the platitudinous mantra, "We become our parents; they become our children"; in other words, parental caregiving is at best role reversal; at worst, a power play. I can only surmise that anyone who repeats such silliness must have fallen for the syllogism, parents make decisions; caregivers make decisions; caregivers are parents. Or perhaps, they bear some latent hostility towards their overbearing parents and relish the opportunity to get even and run their lives.

Even though my mother had dementia and couldn't make reliable, independent, informed decisions in the last four years of her life, she was always "in charge" until she died. I was her surrogate, but I didn't supplant her. I may have *appeared* to be the person making decisions, but I was *always* doing so in accordance with what I knew to be my mother's expressed

Outwardly, the roles of parent and son or daughter may appear to have changed. But the more they actually do, the less caring any caregiver will be. The role of caregiver, I discovered, sometimes the hard way, was always to respect and follow the wishes of my mother — not to treat her like the child I might have thought she became.

wishes and personal sensitivities — with one exception. I would never have put her in a nursing home, with which she herself would have been comfortable, unless I absolutely could not provide an appropriate level of care at home.

Unlike a child, who has not made any responsible, legal, or moral choices in her short life, my mother had made any number of clear and important decisions about her long life, finances, and estate, as long as 18 years before she died. Countless times, she had said, "People are living too long," by which she meant a long life was no life without any real quality of life. For that reason, she made me her healthcare surrogate and signed a living will, indicating she was not to be fed through a tube, resuscitated, or kept alive by extraordinary means.

As she began to fail, in front of doctors, I did my best to keep up the appearance my mother was still in charge of her life. Once, I made the mistake of talking about her with a doctor as though she weren't there. Hurt, she immediately picked up on it and said, "He's in charge now." I apologized and never did it again. From then on, in a typical conversation I always took her feelings into account. A doctor might ask her if she were having trouble swallowing. If she answered a flat-out no, to set the matter straight, I would intervene diplomatically by saying, "But Mother, did I misunderstand? Aren't we seeing the doctor because sometimes it's hard for you to swallow? Am I wrong, but didn't you have trouble the day before yesterday, and didn't we make this appointment so the doctor could help you?" I *always* took the blame for any "misunderstanding" to keep her from being embarrassed. But the doctor would get the point.

As I assumed greater responsibility for my mother's care, first and foremost, my role was to think like my mother and act as I knew she would have acted for herself, not to impose my choices upon her. I couldn't simply tell her what to do, even if I wanted to. Even with dementia, she still had a mind of her own.

When mother went into a rehab facility, the intake nurse asked me if I would approve their giving her medication if she were agitated. But I had already seen too many patients who looked overmedicated and had to take my cue from my mother's strong aversion to prescription medication. Again, deciding as she would have decided for herself, I said absolutely not. If they couldn't handle any agitation she might have without drugging her, I advised her to call us and said we would take her home or find another facility.

Finally, to state the obvious difference between parents raising children and children becoming their parents' caregivers: Parents putting up with the daily frustrations of raising children can rationalize everything from bed-wetting to belligerence because they've got lots to look forward to. They can imagine their infant's growing into a toddler, teen, and young adult with a promising future their whole family happily shares. They can picture holiday celebrations, graduations, weddings, and grandchildren. It's an upward trajectory, filled with hope and optimism.

By sorry contrast, children caring for aging and frail parents face a depressing scenario — a downward spiral, the daily watching of undeniable proof of the loss of independence, mental ability, and physical strength. Parental caregiving amounts to preparing for the worst while desperately trying to make things better — as good as possible, when you know better will never be and good will never be enough.

Parental caregiving is a schizophrenic role for which few, if any of us, are—or can be—fully prepared. But for sure, one thing it isn't is parent-child role-reversal. It's just the reverse of any role we could ever have imagined or thought we'd have to play. The more "children" accept that fact, the better caregivers they'll be.

23

FORGIVING FOLKS
WHO DON'T SEEM TO CARE

Reach out and touch someone.
– Bell System slogan

If truly caring about someone means "being there" for them, no matter what, only my brother and I cared about my mother in her final years. The day-to-day caring *for* her fell more to me, because that had been the plan behind her moving in with me. But emotionally, we both cared equally and deeply *about* her. Watching her slow decline was harder on him than it was on me. Because I saw it every day, I hardly noticed. But even if he visited her after just a few days, the change in her condition shocked him. He never said so, but I could read the pained expression on his face.

If the shoe had been on the proverbial other foot, my mother would never have abandoned friend or relative. Pick a reason, any reason, she had always "been there" for any number of them. But during the last four years of her life, many of them died or became infirm. Those still "with it" who were alive gradually stopped phoning her, once they realized she probably didn't know who they were. I confess I resented people to whom my mother had been kind and generous but who weren't there for her or never even called me to find out how she was.

Typically, people will say they simply don't know what to do or how to relate to someone with dementia or worse. And I can understand their confusion and frustration at one level. But excuses don't get you off the hook, at least not with me. One close friend sadly told me she stopped calling after my mother asked her to spell her name. *So what?* I thought. My mother knew she was talking to someone who cared enough to reach out to her. Her "close" friend could have kept calling to show just how much she *really* cared — and spelled her name however many times, even if it seemed eerie to do so. There would have been no harm in trying.

Before one of my mother's friends stopped calling me to inquire about her, I always told her about our conversations. I'd say so-and-so called to say she loves you. I'd repeat her name again and again. Then, I'd mention her husband's name and her children's name, along with a long list of experiences they shared. Sometimes, I can honestly say I appeared to get through to her. At least, it was worth a try — and there was absolutely no harm done. As ludicrous as my effort may appear, I will always believe some part of people with dementia and related conditions at the very least responds to

I realize now I should have become an assertive caregiver and called people my mother knew but who weren't making the effort to contact her. I should have asked them to call her and volunteered to run interference between them when they did. I could have told her who was on the other end of the phone, especially if they alerted me ahead of time. Who knows what sympathetic chord the sound of a once-familiar voice might have struck in her subconscious. At the very least, she would have sensed someone cared about her. Her friend could have put her bruised ego aside, for that's what got in her way, and made my mother's needs her priority. If she really cared, she would have found a way to remain in touch, and it would have made a major difference, especially in the last months of my mother's life.

once-familiar sounds. And I don't think anyone can disprove me with absolute certainty.

I should have encouraged more people to visit and explained how their presence would have mattered. I could have told them what to do, because I now realize they had no idea. For example, they could have just held my mother's hand and talked to her. It didn't matter whether she appeared to know them or not. For sure, the warmth she felt from their hands together would have made her happy. She responded to me that way and could easily have related to them as well. In the end, it was their loss they chose to be distant. Deep down, I'm sure they know they failed her. And they missed the opportunity of a lifetime to bring the essence of a real relationship to a whole new level.

One of our relatives was in a mild state of shock when he came to see us after an absence of about six months and, as though he were a perfect stranger, my mother, as friendly as she could be, approached him with her hand extended to shake his, saying, "I'm Sylvia Goldstein." I guess it was too much for him to spend time with a perfectly pleasant person, who just happened no longer to recognize him. He could have befriended her in her altered condition, but once was enough — too much. It was the last time we saw him.

Another relative and his wife came to visit. And when he realized my mother didn't know who he was, he apparently thought he could get through to her by saying his name louder and louder and repeating his childhood nickname — to no avail. They stayed in the area for several days, but never came back. Eventually no one came to visit or called.

If friends and relatives didn't know how to show how much they still cared about my mother, imagine the behavior of strangers. Even the most compassionate people, mostly health professionals, saw her as a lost cause — and not just her, anyone old and appearing to be "out of it." The look in their eyes seemed to say, Don't you see how far gone she is? Why do you keep trying to make her better? Why indeed! I wish I had a photo album and biography of my mother with me at all times to drum into their heads exactly how, during her best years — personally and professionally — that "lost cause" could have run circles around them and would never have given up on them. To her, everyone was an object of love.

Relatives, friends, and strangers — even the most caring people too often see old people just as bags of bones, shriveled and demented, in no way beautiful. The face of physical decline scares them. Perhaps, they see in others the frightening reality they fear may await them. In any event, these days, people define beauty in such shallow ways, they are terrified even at the sight of harmless wrinkles. But the way I saw it, the lines on my mother's face came from knitting her brow when she worried about me or from smiling because of something my brother accomplished. Her lines recorded the history of her lifetime of love for her family and friends — a greater gift than getting a facelift and looking silly at 70 trying to look 50.

When my mother no longer recognized people or didn't know their name, they probably took it as rejection at some level. But genuine caring is not about what someone does for you, but what you can do for someone. And there's a four-letter word for it. My mother always remembered her Aunt Alice's favorite song was "How to Handle a Woman" from Camelot. The lyrics advise, "Simply love her, love her, love her." That's all my mother needed from everyone who didn't seem to care about her, what she would have lavished on them had they been in her situation — and why and how she would have forgiven them, whether they ever made the effort to stay in touch with her, or not.

Anyone and everyone can show they care, if they really do. I wrestled with how I could reach out and be in touch with a friend of mine suffering from Alzheimer's who had moved far from me. I knew she was too far gone for us to converse on the phone and no one was with her who could serve as an intermediary. And I couldn't visit her. But one day, I found the perfect solution: sending flowers. She absolutely loved them. Her house was always filled with them. She had tablecloths and throws covered with flowers.

I called the assisted living facility where she stays and told them my flowers would be coming. Of course, a card went with the arrangement with a note expressing my love. But I knew my friend couldn't understand the message — or at least couldn't appear to. I told the people caring for her I understand the seriousness of her condition and I didn't care about her not knowing I sent the flowers. I just wanted her to have something cheerful to look at. The second time I sent an arrangement, the person who brought them to her told me she had actually smiled when she saw them. She also added how significant that was because she rarely smiled.

My mission was accomplished. I send flowers regularly. I don't care if she doesn't know who sends them — or at least appears not to know. I don't care if she can't, or appears not to, understand my message. I only care about bringing a smile to her face — and having finally found a way to show I continue to care about her, and always will.

24

NOT BEING STRONG ENOUGH TO ASK FOR HELP

Help, I need somebody,
Help, not just anybody,
Help, you know I need someone,
Help!
– The Beatles

It's in my DNA to "go it alone," never to ask anyone for help. For that reason, I made a big mistake I wouldn't want anyone else to make: I wasn't strong enough to ask or arrange for any major, regular help taking care of my mother until she was bedridden and in (what turned out to be) her final decline.

Slowly but surely, I accommodated myself to my mother's needs without realizing the toll it was taking on me. Because I work at home, for the better part of every day, I was with her anyway. Devoting my life full-time to providing care came on so gradually, I hardly noticed it was costing me *my* life. Not martyrdom, but inertia and overprotection led me to fall into the trap of round-the-clock caregiving, seven days a week without regular respite.

For most of the time my mother lived with me, we both went about our business independently. Our lives fell into a safe, predictable, mutually supportive pattern. But eventually, for the better part of six years, I gave up going out at night whenever I wanted to, especially after one time when she blew up because I had done so. It was the path of least resistance, and proof positive no good deed goes unpunished.

I had noticed my mother became increasingly annoyed if I left for the evening. She was too proud ever to say she was afraid of being alone. But I figured it was the reason and certainly understood. I thought I came up with an ideal solution when I arranged for my housekeeper, Mrs. Helen Vinson, to stay with her. They had known each other for years and had always been warm and friendly towards each other. I hoped I could get both of them used to being together, my mother would have a new friend, and I'd be able to come and go as I pleased. Wrong!

Helen arrived one Saturday evening, which I hoped would be the first of many, prepared to make dinner for the two of them and spend the evening. I left thinking I found a win-win for us all. But when I returned, the usually cheerful Helen was sitting in the kitchen watching TV, not nearly as upbeat as she was when I left. My mother, alone in her room, was visibly angry. "What is *she* doing here?" she asked me. "I thought you would enjoy her company while I was out," I replied. "I don't need anyone to baby-sit me," she answered, pursing her lips, about as furious as I'd ever seen her. From then on, the *only* person I could get her to accept staying with her was my brother. He'd come to make dinner and spend the evening with her, the only way I was able to go out. He would have relieved

I realized too late I had to avoid making abrupt changes in our daily lives that in any way suggested my mother was no longer in control and able to care for herself. I should have gradually phased in Helen's spending the evening with her. Instead of leaving the first time, I should have stayed with them several times before attempting to go off on my own. Perhaps then, mother would eventually have gotten used to Helen's being there and might even have relished having someone besides me to talk with.

me whenever I asked him to, but I tried not to impose upon him, unless it was absolutely necessary, because he had a number of family and professional responsibilities.

For the last four-and-a-half years of my mother's life, she was my number one priority--24/7/365. There was no number two, or three, or four. My life *completely* revolved around her. Almost imperceptibly, things changed: She became more and more dependent upon me, though still able to attend to her personal needs. The woman who always prided herself on her cooking, especially her baked chicken, and who entertained a steady stream of guests in her home could no longer even toast and butter her morning bagel or brew her cup of tea. I began to do everything for her.

Eventually, for the better part of four years, as my mother's dementia set in, I rarely went out even during the day — and then, only when someone else stayed: my brother or Helen whose presence my mother would gladly accept, as long as she wasn't alone with her at night. I even arranged for someone to come to my house to cut my hair so I wouldn't have to leave her. I tried to get my mother to let him cut hers, but she refused the first time, trusted him only once afterwards, and then flat-out said never again.

The woman who relished completing crossword and word jumble puzzles could no longer do so. She couldn't write checks or balance her checkbook. She could no longer understand what she was reading. I was afraid if I left her alone, she would wander outside, open the door for a stranger who might harm her, or set the house on fire. Only once, she left a burner on high on the stove. But once was enough. I never said anything to her, because she would have been offended, but I always checked the stove after that. At most, if just the two of us were at home, I would steal away for a few minutes to do errands, but only if she was napping.

For the better part of four years, I never had a full night's sleep. I became an ultra-light, fitful sleeper. Every night, I got up multiple times to check on her. I realize only now, after my mother's death, in the final months of her life, I gradually fell into a state of mild depression. I was physically and mentally exhausted.

I didn't ask or arrange for anyone to help me regularly care for my mother so I could go grocery shopping or take a nap without worrying about her. It wasn't anybody else's fault. It simply never occurred to me to get a break from my routine, which was a major mistake. When I finally arranged for help, it was daily, round-the-clock care, but by then she was dying—and I chose not to be away from her for long for any reason.

I learned the hard way that caregivers' first obligation is to take care of themselves — or they won't be able to take care of anyone else. It's sound advice I would give everyone, the same logic airlines follow in the event of the loss of cabin pressure. Adult passengers traveling with children are instructed to put on their masks first; otherwise, they might lose consciousness and wind up unable to help their kids. It isn't weakness to ask for help: It's being strong and the only way to remain so.

25

GETTING *REAL* RESPITE
WITHOUT TAKING ANY TIME OFF

I slept, and dreamed that life was Beauty;
I woke, and found that life was Duty.
— Ellen Sturgis Hooper

There's a finite, physical side to caregiving — a beginning, middle, and end to any number of defined tasks: cooking meals, changing linen, taking someone to a doctor's appointment, going out for a drive. Of course, more than one person can do those things. As time-consuming as they can be, they are the *easy* part of caregiving. They are perfunctory and don't require emotional energy. From that level of caregiving, I could have gotten respite — if my mother had not refused to let anyone other than me, or my brother, be with her, let alone assist her, and if I had not given in to her and found a better way to manage our daily lives.

I could never get respite from the mental side of caregiving by simply finding a way to get some time off or out or away. It was an all-consuming preoccupation I couldn't simply switch on and off. I couldn't take a holiday. No

Respite is not a matter of geography. I couldn't achieve it simply by absenting myself and thinking I could get refreshed. Ultimately, the only real respite came from attaining a certain, almost indescribable, level of acceptance of my caregiving role when I was completely absorbed in it — which is easier said than done.

one else could have relieved my mental pressure. My mother was *always* on my mind. I didn't see myself as simply a caretaker, passively observing my mother's condition. I was constantly trying to discover ways to make her strong and healthy, to reverse the slow ebbing away of her vitality.

Sometimes people would ask me if I were getting any respite, their subtle message being I should, of course. They implied I owed it to myself to get some recreational time. I know they meant well, but their suggestion revealed just how much they were clueless about what I was going through. What could I possibly have done that wouldn't have been the equivalent of meaningless busy work? One person advised me to get some exercise, see people or walk around a mall. But did she think I relished looking in store windows, when buying anything was the furthest thing from my mind while I was watching my mother's life fade away? Someone suggested I see a movie. But an hour or two's worth of diversion wouldn't do it for me. Yet another well-wisher encouraged me to go away for a few days, but all I would have done was worry and call home to be sure mother was okay.

No, escapist, time-off respite wouldn't have worked for me. The few times I did go out naively thinking I could get "relief," I went to small dinner parties. But, to my dismay, I discovered being away actually made coming home and seeing my mother highly emotional for me, even after just a couple of hours. Being with people who were leading average lives made me see how far from normalcy mine was. Sadly, even after being absent for so short a time, with "fresh" eyes, I could see just how much my mother had declined.

No, *real* respite came for me, not when I was running away from caregiving, but when I was in the thick of it. It was vicarious — when for a brief moment, or longer, my *mother* got relief, laughed, and appeared to feel better. Sometimes, I was the cause of it because an ointment I applied took away pain from some part of her body — and she was in seventh heaven. Sometimes, it was because she was no longer anxious after I put a Band-Aid on a bleeding cut on her wrist. Yes, something that simple! At other times, our collective relief came out-of-the-blue in what appeared moments of laughter and joy over something on TV or because she relished something she was eating. My best respite came from my mother's upbeat moments. Those shared experiences were all I needed to refresh me.

Of course, my moments of *real* respite were fleeting and totally unpredictable, just like life itself, which made me appreciate them — and the rewards of being there for my mother — all the more.

The best way I can think of for caregivers to achieve mental respite on-the-job is to keep a journal. I purposely did not, because I knew I would someday write about my experience and I didn't want to influence how I was caring for my mother or describing it because I thought it would later make good copy. More than anything, I didn't want to steal off and jot down observations, as though I were watching a laboratory rat. Finally writing the book I planned has served as a catharsis for me — an extended respite. For other caregivers, keeping a journal would be a sure way to laugh, vent, rail, celebrate — and say things they couldn't say to anyone else, clear their mind, and put everything they are going through in perspective.

26

EXCHANGING ONE SELF
FOR ANOTHER

In search of my mother's garden,
I found my own.
– Alice Walker

I was brought up to believe I mattered — and not just mattered, but *really* mattered. I marched to the beat of the first words of the Three Musketeers: "All for one." I thought everyone in the world was put there for me, myself, and I. It was pretty much my mother's doing. And yet, over a 10 year period, smack in the middle years of my life, I was transformed into someone who did a 180 and gave *his* all for one.

It's the duty of every Jewish mother to make her son, especially her first-born son, think he's special — not to rest until the rest of the world is wise enough to discover it for themselves, and to help them along if they don't, even if it takes them her lifetime to "get it." They resist at their peril — or at least supreme discomfort.

My mother not only fulfilled

Caregiving can be life-transforming if you're open to it, which isn't easy. As I watched my mother fade and die for real, my "old self" faded and died, too. It is not an experience for the faint-of-heart. I had absolutely no idea the nuts-and-bolts of caregiving could yield something life-changing. But it turned out to be the greatest gift I've ever received.

her duty as my personal promoter par excellence, she did double-duty. By her words and deeds, I was given every reason to feel unique. An infant when my father was away during the Second World War, I stayed with her at my grandparents, a staging area for doting if there ever was one. In picture after picture of me in my earliest years, it's clear which son was the center of the universe.

My being in the spotlight only continued and intensified as I grew older. I grew up in New England, where warm pants were a must in winter and gray flannel pants were either a commonly accepted status symbol or my mother's personal choice for social preeminence. I never figured out which.

I couldn't have been more than five years old when I was fitted for my first, of many, pairs of gray flannel pants. Mother took me to a very expensive, "downtown," clothing store. I can still see myself standing in front of a three-paneled mirror while a tailor measured me and the pants legs for cuffs. Back then, pants had to have cuffs! To my mother's chagrin, the flannel caused a rash and made me itch. But undaunted, she had the store sew in a special lining to buffer me from the offending fabric. Nothing was going to keep her from seeing me fulfill my sartorial destiny.

During my mother's lifetime feeding of my self-confidence, if someone disappointed me, she would say, "It's their loss." If something didn't turn out exactly as I wanted it to, she would say, "Something better will come along. If it's meant to be, it's meant to be." What's more, she did everything in her power to allow me to fulfill myself and realize my talents. Displaying an incredible degree of trust in my judgment, she always gave me the opportunity to discover the difference between what I *thought* I wanted and what I *really* wanted. And once I knew what I *really* wanted, she and my father made sure I had whatever resources and encouragement I needed to succeed.

I was already taking classical piano lessons when my parents paid for additional lessons from a second teacher who taught chord improvisation. From him, I learned the tricks of creating my own arrangements of popular melodies. When I decided (for what reason I can't remember) I wanted to play the cello, my mother went along with my whim, and even took me to a music school to discuss my taking lessons, until I nixed the idea on my own.

How or why I got the idea in my head I should go to New York City by myself for my 14th birthday, I have absolutely no idea. But I was somehow drawn to the city early on, as I have been my whole life. My parents gave me the money so I could take the train by myself from Connecticut, and I spent the day exploring museums and Manhattan, alone, the first of many excursions.

My overabundant self-confidence had a negative side to it, however. The egotism — let's call it what it is — which empowered me as an individual also made me, at least in my own mind, unfit to be in a relationship with anyone else. It wasn't as though I actually thought of myself as unfit; I just acted that way. I sacrificed all personal relationships to achieving my goals. No one stood in my way. More broadly speaking, since I had turned all the support I had been given into conditioning myself to believe I was the *only* person who mattered, I never thought I could or *should* "be there" for anyone else. And I wasn't—at least not for the first 55 years of my life, until I invited my mother to move in with me and was able to commit to caring for her until one of us died.

It is ironic — or perhaps karmic — that the one person in my life who gave me my all-encompassing sense of self more than anybody should also have been the one who taught me how to give it up to be there for her — and to prove to myself that I could do it. Of course, by the time I learned it, she didn't consciously teach me such a definitive life-lesson. Nor did I ever feel under any obligation or think of my committing to caregiving as in any way repaying a debt. I simply knew for me, at my stage and position in life, being there completely for her was the *only* thing to do.

Once I became emotionally convinced I wanted my mother to move in with me, the successful outcome of that decision was guaranteed — because, like everything else out of which I made a success, it was what I *really* wanted. I absolutely knew I could do it with the same certainty I absolutely knew I had to go to New York on my own and I should stick to the piano and forget the cello. Though it was a far more significant decision, it came from the same place in my gut, or wherever.

My transformation did not happen all at once, which is perhaps why it was successful. Had I lost too much of my original me suddenly, the shock might have been too much to bear. Gradually, as the years wore on and we lived together, I took a backseat to my self-absorbed self and redirected it outward. And I was able effortlessly to apply the spirit of the words of the Three Musketeers, "all for one," to my circumstances, gladly giving *my* all for one. I replaced all of my personal priorities with those having to do with caring for my mother — literally wiped the board of everything. And, in the process, she gave me the greatest gift of all — selflessness, or the best that I could do to approach it. Only this time, in the ultimate irony of both our lives, she couldn't understand she had given me the greatest gift ever — or could she?

27

PASSING A CRASH COURSE IN UNCONDITIONAL LIVING AND DYING

O Death, where is thy sting?
– Sir Ronald Ross

Shortly after my mother moved in with me, I got a crash course in unconditional love. In the final weeks of her life, I got a crash course in unconditional living and dying. In some ways, I had been preparing for it my whole life; in others, it was a series of fresh revelations.

A friend of mine who had helped start a hospice told me that once you've been on "a death watch," you're never the same. I discovered no truer words have ever been spoken. Intellectually, I had faced the stark reality of my mother's death long before it occurred. But with it staring me in the face, I was unable to fully grasp what was happening. I had no concept of finality — that there would actually be a time when she would breathe her last breath, there would be no turning back, no recoverable moment, and she would be gone forever. When she died, I experienced the shattering reality of the otherwise trite observation that life and death are separated by a single breath and there is a point of no return. Until then, I had lived in a dream world.

My mother died during a period of about seven weeks. Before then, she had been declining slowly, almost imperceptibly, for most of four years. But, after her minor stroke, I could see her life was undeniably ebbing out of her. I lived with the fear of her dying almost all my life after an incident that traumatized me as a child. By the time it was actually happening I was emotionally dead even while deeply grieving.

The process of coming to terms with my mother's death actually began about 60 years before she was on her deathbed, when I was, I'd guess, four or five. We were visiting one of her cousins, a large, ugly beast of a woman. All I can remember is her being almost in my face and saying, "Your mother's going to die," and my shouting, "No, no." I have absolutely no recollection of how the subject of death could possibly have come up. Nor do I remember anything my mother said at the time. But I think it may have been something like "Everybody dies" or "I'm here now, and I won't leave you. Don't worry." Small comfort: For years, I was haunted by the look of that hideous gargoyle of a woman and the terror she instilled in me.

But oddly enough, by the time my mother *was* dying, I no longer feared her doing so. Perhaps, it had been scared out of me as a child. Perhaps, I had simply rationally come to terms with my childhood anxiety in the course of accepting not just my mother's inevitable death, but everyone's, including my own. It had been a haunting memory and a devastating lesson, but it served me well, for I overcame it. In those last weeks, my life felt more surreal than sad, almost like an out-of-body experience — watching myself watching myself watching her, completely detached. Realizations about living and dying came at me fast and furious, as though my mother, even as she was fading from consciousness, were directing them and saying, "Pay attention, because this is the last time I'm going to be able to teach you anything."

My mother forced me to laugh at life during the extended time she was fading. As heart-wrenching and poignant as her last days were, some of the funniest moments of her life occurred in her final weeks — compliments of her. She was a very funny lady. She didn't tell jokes, but her ironic outlook on life fueled her judgments of the world around her in a critical, but compassionate, way. When she was in a rehab facility, even with dementia, she had enough presence of mind to see there were many way-out people around her. Using her typical, incisive, social radar, she'd look at me, cock her head, roll her eyes and, speaking Yiddish so others might not catch on, she'd say, "*Gib a kuk.*" Interpretation: Steal a glance at the craziness over there, but don't let anyone see you. At another time, she was an integral part of the craziness, but still made me laugh. Seated with my mother at a table in the "activities" room, another woman at the rehab center tore pages out of a magazine, then handed them to my mother, who crumpled them into balls and threw them into a wastebasket. I was long past crying or being shocked at such a sight; I simply chuckled at the absurdity of it. Plus, it looked like good therapy for hand-eye coordination. And who was I to judge, anyway? They seemed happy as larks. And I didn't hear anyone else say, "*Gib a kuk*"!

The greatest lesson caregiving for my mother taught me was how to live without regret. She had died slowly, not just in her final weeks, but for several years. Because I had been with her all that time, I was able to say everything to her I could have imagined and do everything for her she needed. My relationship with her was complete.

My mother also made me face harsh realities while she was dying. I couldn't turn away from devastating pictures of her reduced to an object of clinical attention: nurses huddled over a near-lifeless body, a dresser top covered with lotions and rubber gloves, diapers and an oxygen tank waiting in reserve — undeniable proof a once-vital life was reduced to passivity. She had a battalion of people around her caring for her every need — some days as many as five different health professionals. I watched her gradually lose the fight in her and surrender to their attentions, something in better days she would have vigorously fought. There was no way to sugarcoat it.

Too many people never learn hell is paved with good intentions. Too many people at funerals vow they will seize future moments. But they always revert to behaving as though there's *always* another day. A few weeks after my mother died, one of her friends called me to find out how she was doing. Because I didn't know her phone number, I hadn't been able to call her. With genuine regret, she told me she had been waiting to phone my mother on her birthday. I couldn't help but think, *How could you stand on ceremony and wait to call someone who could have died at any moment? Why didn't you spare yourself such avoidable regret?*

I wept when my mother died, but not only because of her dying. Mostly, I wept four-and-a-half years' worth of tears I suppressed as I watched her fade. As devastated as I was when she died, I had been conditioned to accept it, not only because of what she taught me in her final days, but also because of her beastly cousin and the harsh reality she inflicted on me so many years before. Somewhere in the deep recesses of my psyche I must know the reason why she told a mere child his mother would die. Perhaps, we were paying her a condolence call because her young son had drowned. And perhaps, she was still so consumed with grief, she had lost all perspective and didn't know what she was saying, unable to bear seeing a living son with his mother.

Whatever the reason or reasons, two entirely different women, 60 years apart, conditioned me to embrace life unconditionally, so the one death I dreaded for my lifetime would lose its sting.

28

ACHIEVING *MY* CAREGIVING FROM *WITHIN*

Spread your wings.
– Sylvia K. Goldstein

My final reflection on my personal caregiving is about the struggle I've gone through to care for *myself* after my mother's death. For once, her sage advice took longer than usual to work its wonders.

She said, "Spread your wings," decades ago, when I had a chance to work for a year in the Far East after I finished graduate school. After I spent nine years earning three degrees — a bachelor's, master's, and Ph.D — I was offered a position teaching throughout Asia for the University of Maryland. I first dismissed the opportunity as out-of-the-question and would have opted for a traditional job. But when I asked my mother what she thought, she didn't hesitate for a minute. In addition to saying "spread your wings," she added, "You've studied hard all those years, now see the world." I followed her advice. For what turned out to be three years — one in the Far East, two in Europe — I traveled and/or taught in 22 foreign countries. It was a definitive experience, coming at a perfect time in my life: I had finished my studies and was, indeed, as free as the proverbial bird.

A few weeks after my mother died, a friend of mine was embarking on what was for him an exciting, professional adventure. He had made his decision and was all set to go. But to help him overcome his concern for traveling far away from home for a year, I repeated my mother's "spread your wings" advice — and broke down, unable to speak. It was the first time I thought of the phrase in years. Right then, at the same time I was dispensing good advice from my well of memory, with her help, I realized I needed to follow it. But I was stuck.

At various times during mother's final weeks, knowing I would soon be alone, I wondered what I'd be facing and how I'd adjust. I foolishly thought I would get closure after my brother and I scattered her ashes at sea in the exact spot where my father's ashes were placed 18 years before. But even the symmetry of that experience didn't bring me peace and comfort me.

The isolation of caregiving can be totally liberating in ways I could never have imagined. Most people typically fill their time out of habit and carry a lot of excess baggage. I certainly did. But during my isolation, I discovered who my friends really were and what was really important to me. I realized how much psychic energy I had wasted on people who didn't care about me. Eventually, I was able to sort out my priorities and decide on whom and on what I would expend my energy in the future.

Shortly after she died, it occurred to me to go out at night, not having done so for the better part of four years. I got in my car and drove off guardedly, as though I were on a reconnaissance mission to see what an unknown world was like. I literally couldn't believe so many people were out and about. I asked myself, *What are they doing? Where were they going?* I felt like someone who had arrived from another planet, and in some ways I was.

One thing immediately became clear to me: I had to molt before I could spread my wings. I didn't want my old life back, especially with all its illusory freedom. But I wasn't sure what new life I was embracing.

Finally, I have only been able to "spread my wings" and give myself a strong dose of caregiving by writing this book, by achieving *my* caregiving from *within*: reliving every thought, emotion, and incident I could remember and recreate — and sharing them with others. I am writing these final words and actually finished this book on August 11, on what would have been my mother's birthday and on what now feels like my rebirth day.

29

CAREGIVING OF EVERYONE, BY EVERYONE, AND FOR EVERYONE

*You cannot imagine the kindness I've received
at the hands of perfect strangers.
– W. Somerset Maugham*

Everywhere, I see elderly people, especially women, who appear to need someone to take care of them. One frail-looking woman using a walker — I'd guess in her 80's — was ahead of me, struggling to get through the front door of an office building. In several tries, she couldn't manage to move her walker out of the path of the heavy (for her) door so she could open it far enough to get in. Of course, I helped her and then held the elevator door until she slowly made her way across the lobby.

About an hour later, when I left the building, this same lady was standing outside in the middle of the sidewalk, gripping her walker, and looking from side to side at approaching vehicles, mildly agitated and confused. When I asked her if she was being picked up, she said yes, but added she didn't know when. I had seen her drive up in a van transporting people who need assistance. When I volunteered to call the service, she showed me the piece of paper on which she had written the phone number in her careful but shaky handwriting.

I reached the dispatcher at 2:50 p.m. and was coldly told the lady was scheduled for pickup between 3:00 and 3:30 p.m. I urged her to send the van as quickly as possible. When I relayed the conversation, the lady said she wasn't feeling well. I asked her where she lived, but since it wasn't anywhere near my house, I didn't offer to drive her there. The truth is, I still had my mother to take care of and had to get home to let the person staying with her leave. The best I could do was to escort the woman back into the lobby, where I left her sitting and waiting for her ride.

My heart broke for that woman. Obviously, I haven't been able to get her out of my mind. She looked to me like everyone's mother or grandmother or favorite aunt. In her, I saw my own mother if she didn't have me to look after her. She was left alone and defenseless, abandoned at least for that time, to fend entirely for herself, using all the mental and physical energy she possessed struggling to go to something as routine as a doctor's appointment, I guessed.

She was beautifully dressed, immaculate, well coifed; she seemed to be mentally sharp. I'm guessing in her younger days, she cared for others impeccably, too. But from all outward appearances, it seems when her time has come, no one is there for her. Of course, I may be wrong. This kind, harmless-looking old woman may really have been or still be a terror; her family may hate her with good reason — she, them. But I don't think so.

Sadly, tragically too many old la-

The odds are you will become an unpaid, family caregiver, if you are not one already. Relish the role. As a society we need to train more paid, professional caregivers, but nothing should take the place of families caring for their own. These days, all the talk about health care and insurance focuses on the uninsured. But there are untold numbers of seniors who don't only need medical care but help with day-to-day living — along with that indefinable of all things, someone to love them and treat them like a human being, the kind of attention which everyone deserves and for which no one should have to ask.

dies on walkers — and let's not forget the men — are left to walk alone. They have grown old and old old, older than anyone thought likely or planned for. As most will attest, no one wants you when you're old and infirm — unless you've got lots of money and are going to leave it to them; and even then, they're likely to want to park you out of sight and mind and make sure you don't spend all of their inheritance.

Old people should be living with their families. No one should be left to "depend on the kindness of strangers." The world is too cold and ugly, and there are too many doors almost impossible for some people to open — but so easy for others.*

*The original version of this story was first published as one of my op-ed columns in the Sun-Sentinel on March 26, 2008.

30

DETERMINING YOUR "CAREGIVER READINESS": *POST*-ASSESSMENT

An ethic of care rests on the premise
of nonviolence — that no one should be hurt.
– Carol Gilligan

Now, complete your "Caregiver Readiness" *Post*-Assessment. It's exactly like your *Pre*-Assessment. Before scoring yourself again, read the tip below each benchmark to refresh your memory about the issues you'll face as a caregiver. Don't look at your *pre*-assessment scores until you've completed your *post*-assessment and have followed the directions for doing so.

Of course, I hope in the course of your reading you will have transformed yourself, to your own satisfaction, into a ready, able, and informed caregiver. If you've taken the *pre*-assessment, read the entire book, and are willing to take the *post*-assessment and compare the results of both assessments, you are surely well on your way to being a model family caregiver.

But as you have no doubt realized by now, your attitude towards caregiving will largely determine how successful you are, much more than your skill and knowledge in carrying out given tasks. And attitudes take time to change. Go easy on yourself. Give yourself the time you need to evolve into a rational caregiver by being committed to the process, which may mean retaking the *post*-assessment and comparing results from time to time.

Scoring Your "Caregiver Readiness"
Post-Assessment

On a scale from 0 (not at all) to 10 (absolutely), circle your score in response to each of the following statements:

....

1. I have thought through all the pros and cons of assuming the responsibility for caregiving 0 1 2 3 4 5 6 7 8 9 10

Before you score yourself, divide a sheet of paper into two vertical columns. Mark one Pros and under it list everything you can think of that would make you *want* to take responsibility for caregiving. Under Cons, list everything you can imagine that would make you *not want* to become a caregiver. For example, in what column(s) would you put how you feel about the people for whom you might be caring? If you hate your mother, you'd be in for a bumpy ride, unless you can harness your negatives. You need to be very clear about how you score this benchmark. Unless your family member is clearly fading fast, your caregiving may extend into months or years. Are you willing to take one day at a time for however long it may be? If you don't give yourself a 10 here, you may be taking on a commitment which will potentially ruin your life and shortchange your family member.

What would you be willing to do to improve your score?_

_____

_____

_____

2. I am willing to make caregiving my number one priority, when and if the need arises 0 1 2 3 4 5 6 7 8 9 10

Before you determine your score, write down all the priorities in your life, from major to minor. Where would you place caregiving?

What would you be willing to do to improve your score?

_____

_____

_____

3.   I am willing to discuss all the issues involved in my role as caregiver with all of my family members who need, or may need, my help 0 1 2 3 4 5 6 7 8 9 10

Before you give yourself a 10 or less, list everyone you need to talk with, as well as what issues you need to discuss and what questions you need to ask and answer. Your conversation needs to be no-holds-barred. For example, you should address everything from how they see you as caregiver to under what circumstances you might end your role and place your family member in a nursing home or other facility or under someone else's care.

What would you be willing to do to improve your score?

_____

_____

_____

4.   I am willing to provide a separate living space for my family member within my home 0 1 2 3 4 5 6 7 8 9 10

Score yourself only after you ask yourself if *you* would want to live in the space you would make available to your family member. Are you prepared to redecorate it as your family member might want it? Are you willing to go so far as to add additional space onto your home if necessary — or even move into a new house to accommodate her needs? How willing are you to make *your* home feel welcoming?

What would you be willing to do to improve your score?

_____

_____

_____

5. I will see to it that all necessary papers (living will, healthcare surrogate, will, durable power of attorney, etc.) are executed by my family member(s) to ensure I am able to carry out my role as caregiver........... 0 1 2 3 4 5 6 7 8 9 10

There is nothing perfunctory about signing such important papers. Before you determine your score, think of the profound issues that creating and signing these few papers will raise. You will be asking your family members to put in writing who gets what from their estate, as well as when a machine keeping them alive would be shut off — or not.

What would you be willing to do to improve your score?

_____

_____

6. I understand I can't be a caregiver by myself, and I need to create my own support system to help me ....
0 1 2 3 4 5 6 7 8 9 10

Before you rate yourself, list all of the current needs of your family member(s), as well as others you think are likely. Next, list all of the things you can think of you may need to do as a caregiver. Then, underline all of the things you believe *only* you can and should do. Next, make a list of people who might make up your support system. Next to their names put the responsibilities you believe they could handle exclusively or share. For example, next to someone's name you might suggest she commit to taking your family member to doctors' appointments or giving you a night off or taking your place while you go shopping. You may list the same responsibility next to more than one name. Do you have more needs than names (whoops!), or the reverse (lucky you!)?

What would you be willing to do to improve your score?

_____

_____

_____

7. I am willing to plan for the financial resources to cover my family member's caregiving needs ....
0 1 2 3 4 5 6 7 8 9 10

Caregiving is costly both in time and money. Before you give yourself a 10, make a list of all the caregiving scenarios you can think of (your family member completely at home, possibly needing to go to a rehab facility, eventually choosing to go into a nursing home, whatever). Then, write down the financial implications of each alternative. List all available financial resources. For example, next to your at-home scenario, consider the possible cost of having to bring in temporary or long-term outside help. Compare the costs and benefits of long-term health insurance. Consider the cost-benefit of someone in your family not working, but making caregiving a full-time job. If your potential support system is extensive, consider actually pooling resources and paying a family member to provide care, instead of working elsewhere.

What would you be willing to do to improve your score?

_____

_____

_____

8. I am willing to create a family caregiving strategy after conferring with other family members ....
0 1 2 3 4 5 6 7 8 9 10

I hope you would rate yourself a 10 at this point, because that's really where you need to be in your thinking. Once you have determined (1) what your family member's caregiving needs are and are likely to become, (2) what your responsibilities and needs are, (3) who the members of your support group are, (4) what you think you can and should depend upon others for, and (5) what the cost of caregiving is likely to be, develop a DRAFT written plan for everyone potentially involved to discuss.

What would you be willing to do to improve your score?

_____

_____

_____

9. I am willing to be an advocate for my family members so they get the care to which they are entitled.................................
0 1 2 3 4 5 6 7 8 9 10

Before you circle a number, ask yourself if you have the stamina, smarts, and diplomatic skills to ensure your family member always receives the care she deserves and is entitled to. For example, are you willing to become thoroughly familiar with what your insurances cover and don't cover, even before you may need to file a claim? Forewarned is forearmed. Negotiating the labyrinth of prescription drug formularies can be frustrating — and costly. Most of all, are you willing to speak up to doctors and other health care professionals to ensure they are caring for your family member in the best possible way — and keeping you informed about options and decisions you need to weigh? You'll need to do all of the above, and more, and still keep your cool, "speaking softly, but carrying a big stick," to be most effective. How well do you think you can do the job?

What would you be willing to do to improve your score?

_____

_____

_____

10. I am prepared to see to it my family member receives appropriate medical and dental services and attention ....
0 1 2 3 4 5 6 7 8 9 10

Assuring proper medical attention for an aging family member, especially one with dementia or similar condition, is obviously crucial for his well-being. It's sometimes far more difficult than you might imagine, however. Going to doctor's and dentist's appointments is easy, though it obviously takes time you and others in your support group will have to make available. But your family member may decide he doesn't want to leave the house to keep an appointment. She may even tell you she doesn't want to see anymore doctors or dentists. You can't allow them to harm themselves by refusing the care they need. If you absolutely can't get them to a doctor or dentist, you may need to find a way to bring medical services into your home, for which you may have to pay out-of-pocket. Be prepared, and understand that you absolutely cannot shirk such an important responsibility. You've got to guarantee they'll get the care they need--and score a 10 here!

What would you be willing to do to improve your score?

_____
_____
_____

Total all your scores to get your "Caregiver Readiness"
_____ out of 100

What might your score mean?
Move on to judge your "Caregiver Readiness."

Judging your "Caregiver Readiness"

On a scale of 0 (terrible) to 10 (great),

....

How do you feel about your score? 0 1 2 3 4 5 6 7 8 9 10

Ways to interpret your score:

Of course, your total score is an obvious way to benchmark how prepared and successful you are likely to be as a caregiver. But far more important are your 10 individual scores and what you would be willing to do to improve each of them.

To repeat: Your attitude towards caregiving is more important than anything else. Someone committed to giving it his all will overcome any difficulty or obstacle. Someone begrudgingly caregiving will put herself through a nightmare. Set yourself up for success: More than anything else, adjust your attitude towards caregiving, before you commit to it.

Compare your *pre*-assessment and *post*-assessment scores:

1. **Pre:** ____ **Post:** ____ **What does the comparison tell you about your caregiving readiness?**_____

_____

What do you think you need to do next?_____

_____

2. **Pre:** ____ **Post:** ____ **What does the comparison tell you about your caregiving readiness?**_____

_____

What do you think you need to do next?_____

_____

3. **Pre:** ____ **Post:** ____ **What does the comparison tell you about your caregiving readiness?**_____

What do you think you need to do next?_____

4. Pre: ___ Post: ___ What does the comparison tell you about your caregiving readiness?_____

What do you think you need to do next? _____

5. Pre: ___ Post: ___ What does the comparison tell you about your caregiving readiness?_____

What do you think you need to do next? _____

6. Pre: ___ Post: ___ What does the comparison tell you about your caregiving readiness?_____

What do you think you need to do next? _____

7. Pre: ___ Post: ___ What does the comparison tell you about your caregiving readiness?_____

What do you think you need to do next? _____

8. Pre: ___ Post: ___ What does the comparison tell you about your caregiving readiness?_____

What do you think you need to do next? _____

---

9. Pre: ____ Post: ____ What does the comparison tell you about your caregiving readiness?_____

What do you think you need to do next? _____

---

10. Pre: ____ Post: ____ What does the comparison tell you about your caregiving readiness?_____

What do you think you need to do next? _____

Reminder:

After you compare your results and determine what's next for you, remember to go to my blog, www.rationalcaregiving.blogspot.com, for updates and information, as well as to email me your comments and questions.

ACKNOWLEDGMENTS

Usually, words don't fail me, but they do here. I have to fall back on basic arithmetic to help me convey the intensity of my thoughts: Whatever thanks I express, multiply by infinity to get an approximation of the real depth and scope of my appreciation for the two sine qua nons in my life.

Without my brother Fred, I couldn't have written this book, because I couldn't have been my mother's caregiver. She could count on me because I always knew that I could count on him. I tried not to burden him with day-to-day issues, because as a lawyer, artist, father, one side of a relationship, and friend to others, he was pulled in many directions. He never said no whenever I needed him and rearranged his life any number of times, without hesitation, even at short notice, when I asked him for help. He's the quiet, steadfast energy behind this book.

Without Bobbe Schlesinger, my friend of more than 30 years, I might not have finished my manuscript by my self-imposed deadline — or written with the assurance that my oh-so personal story would resonate with and help others. Talking with her on the phone one day, I told her that I was making steady progress — and, luckily for me, out-of-the-blue, asked, "Would you like to hear what I've just written?" "Of course!" she answered enthusiastically. That was the first of many readings. A brilliant listener, she helped me immeasurably.

ABOUT THE AUTHOR

Author, journalist, and radio and TV talk show host Stephen L. Goldstein is also a nationally recognized trends analyst and forecaster, and a fundraising and communications executive. He is president and CEO of Educational Marketing Services, Inc. and an op-ed columnist for *The Sun-Sentinel* (*Tribune* paper in South Florida). His columns have also appeared in *The Los Angeles Times, Newsday, The Cleveland Plain Dealer, The San Francisco Chronicle, The Baltimore Sun,* and other leading publications. Goldstein earned his bachelor's, master's and Ph.D. at Columbia University and currently lives in Fort Lauderdale, Florida.